Hello Computer:
The heartfelt story of a woman in tech
by
Linda A Macaulay
ISBN: 978-1-914933-26-4

A copy of this book is deposited with the British Library

Illustrations by Adam Allsuch Boardman

Published By: -

i2i
PUBLISHING

i2i Publishing. Manchester.
www.i2ipublishing.co.uk

Table of Contents

Dedicated to Patrick. My wonderful husband,
co-parent of Jon, Theresa, Christine, and
grandfather of Celeste, Celine,
Frances and Vincent.

Preface

I'll never forget that momentous day in 1967 when I saw my first computer. Aged 17, I was awestruck that a machine could carry out instructions and, what's more, it could carry out *my* instructions. I simply asked it to add two numbers together, told it how to do it and, to my amazement, it displayed the correct answer. I could do it over and over again with different numbers and it was always right. I was hooked for life.

Computers have changed immensely in my lifetime: they've got faster, smaller, more intelligent, and they've become networked and embedded in everyday objects. They have been central to my development and as they have changed, so has my life.

It is my belief that computers have the potential to enhance people's lives if only we can understand how best to keep the needs of humans at the heart of their design.

In fact, I've spent my whole life learning about the interaction between computing technology, which changes constantly and people who, fundamentally, don't change that much.

Early childhood experiences laid the foundation of my values. I learned that you have to be determined and hard-working to make something of yourself.

State education provided the opportunity for me, a working-class girl, to achieve financial independence and ultimately become a professor at one of the top universities in the UK.

I always enjoyed maths at school and the computer's logic fitted with my way of thinking. I learnt scientific programming as an undergraduate. Then, as a postgrad, I studied more technical 'low-level' programming that enabled me to understand the internal workings of the computer itself.

As I grew older, I realised that computers weren't just for science, determining flight paths of spaceships or doing massive calculations, but also had the potential to change people's lives. I became fascinated by how people might use computers and whether those who didn't think in a logical, mathematical way would be able to use them.

My first job in 1973 was in a hospital when computers in wards were still experimental. I was interested in how you could design a system that a nurse could use when tending to patients. It wasn't obvious at all – the computer was a big, heavy machine, too noisy to be taken into a quiet hospital ward. The computer programs followed fixed logical procedures. In contrast, the nurse was more flexible, sensitive and acted intuitively depending on the needs of patients. They were from different worlds – the human on one side and the computer on the other.

I knew how to use the computer to solve a technical problem where no humans were directly involved, but on the ward there would have to be direct interaction between my program and the nurse. There were so many questions to be answered before programming could start: What skills did the nurse have? What training would be needed? What were the aims of the system? What was the best design? How would it fit with the daily routine of the ward round?

As well as using my technical skills, I had to be creative and think of possible new ways of doing the ward round – what the nurse should do, what the computer should do, assess alternative solutions, and understand the nurse as a computer user – before embarking on the design. I learned that user needs must come first, followed by the design and finally the programming.

In another hospital, working with pathologists, I wrote programmes to gather data from various machines, standardise the readings and collate the results into a single report for doctors. From a programming point of view, this was quite straightforward until I realised that if the calculations were wrong and, for example, the report told a doctor that a patient's glucose level was high when in fact it was low, there could be serious consequences: programming errors could have life or death consequences.

I learned that, as a programmer, it's important to be professional and think about the ethics and morality of what you are doing. I thought then and think now that all programmers and designers should have to abide by an ethical code of conduct.

Having said that, it was tremendously satisfying to see the system working in the pathology lab and to see doctors happy that it significantly reduced their associated workload.

It was particularly rewarding working with smaller businesses where I could see the design process through from the first idea or articulation of a problem to the solution.

One company I worked with in the late 1990s sold health products to local gyms. The boss who came to see me was curious about the potential of the internet. I was able to put a team together to investigate what he really wanted and, consequently, to design and build an appropriate e-commerce system. Within two years he went from selling products locally from a small back office to selling across Europe from a large warehouse. His revenue tripled, he employed more staff and within a few years had an enviable revenue growth graph.

The whole project was such fun; my team and I learned about the power of the internet, about web-based programming and about designing for people who knew very little about using computers. We were glad to work with the company owner who had a strong social conscience, often employing young ex-offenders and sponsoring amateur sportsmen and women who needed help to get forward in life.

We felt we had made a positive difference to a local business and, indirectly, to the lives of those associated with it.

One amazing thing about computing and software is the way you can make something out of nothing. I've seen a 9-year-old child create a computer game to teach youngsters about climate change and be excited when she saw people using it. I've helped a women's group create a mobile phone app and have that eureka moment when they saw it working on other people's iPhones.

By telling my story I hope to convey the excitement of working with computers to help improve people's lives, to make a difference in business, to make something out of nothing and to be creative in solving problems.

Learning how to program and how computers work quickly enabled me to understand new technologies. We are still living through the digital revolution and there is a new challenge almost every day.

I endeavoured to learn more about people through psychology, sociology, and behavioural sciences as well as through practice.

Experience has taught me that the human sciences and the computer sciences need to work together to meet the complex needs of users. For me, the meeting point of the two disciplines is in the design of a given system. User needs should be embedded in that design and, ultimately, in the software/hardware itself. Human Computer Interaction and System Design are my passion.

But things were not always easy. I feel that being a woman in a predominantly male profession meant I had to be strategic about my career choices, be skilful in building teams and networks and be determined to create a leadership style that suited me.

Of course, new technologies are not created in a vacuum; they are a reaction to the social and political context of their time.

Technology and data are not neutral and often embody archaic social and political biases. Unfortunately, gender bias remains a problem not only in the computing workforce but also in the way systems are designed.

It is my strong belief that the full potential of computers to enhance people's lives will not be achieved until the gender imbalance in the profession is properly redressed.

I want women to be successful, be more strategic, become leaders and make a positive contribution to the future of tech.

Chapter 1 Where it all started

If it wasn't for the codebreakers at Bletchley Park [1], you probably wouldn't be reading this story. By deciphering coded enemy messages by hand and machine, the codebreakers played a crucial role in bringing the Second World War to an end and, consequently, in my father's survival.

World War II Royal Engineers Corps of the British Army

Dad was in the Royal Engineers Corps of the British Army, stationed in Scotland. One night in 1944 as the war was drawing to a close Dad met Mum at a dance in the local village hall in Carnoustie. He was a handsome young man in uniform, and Mum an auburn-haired young woman in a blue tea dress. They longed to be together. Mum continued to work as an accounts clerk at the local bakery and another year passed before Dad's demobilisation orders were issued.

Mum was 19 and my Dad 24 when they married and, within the year, they had their first child, my elder sister, Sheila. Finding work was a priority and, having found nothing suitable in Carnoustie, they decided to move to my father's hometown of Burnley, Lancashire.

Burnley was a dirty old mill town where the air was a mixture of smoke and fog; if you stood on the hillside above Burnley, you could only see the tops of the factory chimneys, the rest being covered in a thick smog. Carnoustie on the other hand was a lovely seaside town with fresh clean air, sandy beaches and a wonderfully green golf course. Poor Mum!

Though my Dad worked hard as a cabinet maker, his income was barely enough to support the family. I lived with Mum and Dad, my brother and sister - the five of us in a small, terraced house with two bedrooms, an outside toilet and no bathroom. As a young child in the 1950s I would lie in bed before school and hear the clogs of the cotton mill workers on the cobbled streets as they headed for a 6am start. The early morning air was filled with smoke belching from factory chimneys and coal fires in every hearth. I was glad to snuggle down until Mum had lit our fire and it was warm enough to go downstairs.

I never felt poor. My parents were kind and loving. They took us on picnics, walks in the countryside, and showed us how to pick blackberries to sell at our local greengrocer for a little spending money. Dad taught us how to fix things, how to change a light bulb, mend a plug, how to make things from wood, use a ratchet screwdriver, a wood plane and saw. Mum showed us how to peel, chop and cook vegetables, mash potatoes, make cottage pie, salmon rolls, rice puddings, and how to bake cakes and biscuits.

Every Friday, when Dad got paid, we bought fish and chips for tea and fresh cream cakes from the bakery — not very healthy you might think — but delicious and a real treat for Mum, because on Fridays she didn't have to cook.

Mum was a Catholic and took us to church every Sunday morning and then for tea and biscuits in the church hall. If we didn't behave ourselves, Mum would say, "Wait 'til you get home; your Dad will give you a good hiding."

If any of us had been annoyingly naughty, she would tell Dad. We were a bit scared but knew that he wouldn't actually hit us. He would say, "Come into the sitting room and close the door – it's the belt for you, young lady."

Once there, he would take off his leather belt, fold it in half, crack it really loud and say, "Shout as if it hurts - and don't tell your Mum."

Dad was far too kind and loving to smack us – it was our little secret. As we returned to the kitchen, he would say, "Now let that be a lesson to you", and Mum would be satisfied that the deed was done.

In the 1950s, it was fairly normal to hit a child for misbehaving. I was smacked on the legs with a wooden ruler when I was at junior school – once just for not writing a letter F properly, and another time for talking to the girl next to me. I was hit with a slipper if I arrived late for school assembly – one of the teachers would stand halfway up the stairs and catch you on the way up. Relatively speaking, I was a good child, or at least I always believed I was. I wasn't a bully; I was always clean and my clothes were neat and tidy. I wasn't one of the poor kids whose parents didn't care and who came to the school with shaven heads and headscarves because they'd had such bad head lice.

I wasn't a softie either; I learned how to look after myself and who to avoid. I also had a big brother: "I'll get my brother to beat you up", was a last resort – though he was quite protective of me. We played out unsupervised in the street after school – skipping, hopscotch, ball games – always with neighbours' children. I learned to take turns, negotiate until I got what I wanted and learned when to back down and who to trust.

I was guided by my Mum; everyone loved her. She was kind to friends and neighbours and every year helped organise the church jumble sale. It took place in the church hall and everyone brought bags of unwanted clothes to the church in the weeks leading up to it. The helpers, like Mum, set up stalls – one for children's clothes, another for men's coats, bric-a-brac, a bookstall and so on. On the set day local people would queue up to buy things off the stalls – you could buy a dress for sixpence or coat for two shillings.

The idea was to help the poor by selling everything at a low price and at the same time making money for the church. We occasionally bought clothes from there if Mum could find something nice when she was setting up the stalls, but we never got holiday clothes from the jumble sale.

Every summer, we went to the seaside in Carnoustie, Scotland, to stay with Grandma and Grandpa. Mum always wanted us to look especially nice for her mum and dad, so we went shopping in C&A in Manchester before the summer holidays. It was wonderful to buy new dresses, underwear and a new coat. When I was seven, I got my favourite dress ever: a white dress with beautiful pink roses, a big white collar that went all across my shoulders, a thin red belt and wonderful heart-shaped buttons.

It took ages to reach Grandma's, going via Preston-Edinburgh-Dundee-Carnoustie, almost 300 miles. We travelled by coach and steam train and then stayed for the first two weeks of July, which was "Burnley Fair" when mills and factories closed, and everyone had a holiday at the same time.

The first thing I noticed, when we got to Grandma and Grandpa's, was the glorious smell of fresh-baked bread. They ran a small guest house; we were their only guests for our two weeks. The beds were massive, they had a bathroom and a garden and were only 10 minutes' walk from the beach. It was heaven. Grandma would set the table for meals, always with a white linen tablecloth, silver cutlery, silver cruet-set and jam-holder and beautiful dinner and tea sets. Every meal was a treat, though, of course, we had to be on our best behaviour. Grandpa would sit in the garden and smoke a pipe after dinner, and we were allowed to join him and enjoy a peaceful hour before going to bed. We were tired out after spending the whole day outside in the fresh air – on the beach, in the sea, playing crazy golf or running up and down the sand-dunes. Grandpa taught us how to catch crabs among the rocks and take them home for Grandma to cook. She kept them in a big sink with a wooden lid on top, then boiled them alive – all very scary.

I was especially happy to be with Dad. I was his youngest and the baby of the family for seven years. I'd ask him to do everything for me – help me dress, tie my shoelaces, hold my hand. I'd follow him into his workshop; he'd sit me on the bench from where I'd watch him making sewing boxes and small tables which he would sell to the local hardware shop to earn extra money. One time he kept me out of the workshop; he said he was making a surprise and didn't want anyone to see it. At Christmas I was delighted to find that the surprise was for me: a doll's house all made from wood. It had four rooms, a front door, windows, electric lights and even wallpaper, a roof that lifted so you could see into the bedrooms and, best of all, tiny wooden furniture – chairs, a table, two beds, a bath and sink. Mum had sewed little bedcovers and a tablecloth. It was perfect.

When I was 7, my little sister was born. It was a big change for me – I was no longer the baby of the house. I knew that

Mum and Dad wanted to move to a bigger house; they were saving up and had started looking. When the baby came home from hospital, there was no cot for her and no special room. At first, she slept in a drawer from our sideboard – we had a very big sideboard that Dad had made in expectation of moving. Mum, Dad and baby slept in one bedroom, my sister, brother and I slept in the other bedroom. I was 7, my sister 12 and my brother 10. My sister and I shared a double bed and my brother had the single bed. I know it was worse for my older sister because she really needed privacy and somewhere to do her homework.

Mum had to give up her part-time job as a dinner lady at our school to look after the baby and to earn more money Dad changed his job, to become a fitter in an aerospace factory. I didn't see as much of my Dad after that because he worked a three-shift system – sometimes he was home at mealtimes or bedtimes and sometimes he wasn't. We had to keep quiet during the day in case he was sleeping.

. . . then suddenly everything fell apart.

One morning I was lying in bed warm and cosy waiting for Dad to arrive home from his night shift. I listened for the back door to open and as Mum was serving him a cooked breakfast, I ran downstairs to give him a hug.

As I entered the kitchen Mum shouted: "Stop there! Go back upstairs, get your brother - be quick".

I could see that Dad was on the floor - what was the matter? His face was blue. My brother, age 13 appeared.

"Run as fast as you can to the phone box - dial 999 - we need an ambulance".

My heart was racing, what could I do? I sat on the staircase listening. Mum was sobbing and trying to rouse Dad. "Come on Bill, you'll be okay, wake up! wake up!"

The ambulance arrived, they took Dad out on a stretcher, and I never saw him again. No more early morning hugs, no more lying-in bed anticipating his return.

Mum was a widow at the age of 36 and I was 11.

I don't remember crying but I suppose I must have done. Suddenly Dad was gone. Grandma and Grandpa came down from Carnoustie to stay with us for a couple of weeks. Mum was glad of some help but, in the end, she wanted to be on her own and deal with things herself. She was a very strong woman but dreadfully sad; she was heartbroken – Dad was her first and only true love and remained so for the rest of her life.

My father's death was a massive shock. We lived in a small two-bedroomed house with little money and no prospects of moving. The house had a small bathroom that my father had installed in one of the bedrooms, but there was no inside toilet; the toilet was in the back yard. The thing I dreaded most was having to go to the toilet during the night. I'd walk or often slide down the steep staircase to the kitchen, open the kitchen door and see cockroaches crawling across the floor. I'd put the light on, and they would all scurry under the sink. I would run across to the back door as fast as I could, open it, race across the yard to the toilet and then dread the return journey.

I didn't know it then, but bugs of one sort or another were to become a recurring theme in my life.

I had taken my entrance exams for grammar school only weeks before Dad died; he had always really encouraged me, and I was incredibly disappointed that he never found out that I had passed.

We had no income except a small amount by way of the state widow's pension and family allowance. Mum had to go to work full time. A neighbour looked after our little sister and after school we three older children did the household chores and made tea for when Mum got home.

I didn't mind but my older sister, by then 16, found it more difficult because it restricted her freedom. My brother was different because people said, "Oh, now Dad's gone, you're the man of the family", so he got out of doing things and thought it meant he could boss me about. In any case my old life fell apart.

It took us about five years to come to terms with the fact that Dad had died.

I knew life would never be the same again, but you have to be strong when something like that happens. You have to say: look, life has changed, you've still got to make the most of it. I'd just passed my exams for grammar school, and I thought this was an opportunity and what Dad would have wanted me to do. I didn't want to be left penniless like Mum, and she wanted me to get a good job and be able to earn some money. She taught me that if you were financially independent then you had choices: you could decide whether to buy a house, whether to live on your own or with somebody else so that you could have a better life. So, at eleven years old, I knew I had to start my life again.

It was very difficult for my Mum; sometimes she got thoroughly fed up. If she was really down, we set about doing all the household jobs and we didn't complain about anything. We said, "Oh, come on Mum, I'll make you a cup of tea," or "Sit down for a while; it'll be all right, don't worry." She was heartbroken and just couldn't cope — everything was too much. The three of us older children had to rally round and try to make things better for her. As well as being strong yourself you also had to be strong for other people when there was a disaster in the family. You had to support each other in getting through it — so that's what we tried to do.

Amazingly, Mum managed to kit me out for the new school. There was a school uniform shop where she could pay a small amount each week. In summer we had blue dresses, striped blazers and a straw boater, and in winter we had turquoise blouses, pinafores, a brown coat and brown velour hats. The school was particularly fussy that we should wear brown leather lace-up shoes, 60-denier stockings (with seams) and brown knickers. Knickers were inspected in gym classes where, of course, we wore brown gym skirts.

I had to walk about half a mile through the rows of terraced houses and cobbled streets to get to the bus stop for school. You can imagine the reaction of the local kids seeing me in a fancy school uniform; they called me names and had great fun running up behind me and knocking off my hat.

The school was an all-girls Convent Grammar School run by Sisters of Mercy, they had some boarders but we were mostly day girls. We had prayers at morning assembly and stopped whatever we were doing for the Angelus prayer at 12 noon. During Lent, a nun read psalms or scripture to us while we ate lunch. I didn't mind prayers, for at least it was a quiet time. I loved the mid-day meal though; we sat at bench-like tables for eight with a prefect at the top end. The two girls furthest from the prefect had to set the table and bring the tureens of food. I thought it was wonderful to be waited on and have a hot meal cooked for you with meat, potatoes, vegetables and a pudding.

The first few years at grammar school were tricky: I did work hard but at times had a rather bad attitude. For example, our religious education teacher asked us to learn the ten plagues by heart (the ten plagues of Egypt in Exodus). I thought this was unnecessary and refused to do it, so, for punishment, I had to write out the ten plagues 10 times; I didn't do it, so she said I had to write them out 50 times and I didn't do that either. When it got to a 100 and tempers were becoming frayed, I decided I would do it, and came in next day with the ten plagues written out one hundred times. I've no idea how many I actually wrote, but when I took them out to the teacher in front of the class, she just tore them up in my face and put them in the bin. To this day I have no idea what the ten plagues are.

I loved physics though; the physics teacher would ask us interesting questions such as, "If you are lying down in a bath of water and start moving around, will the water get hotter or colder?" Others looked perplexed but, to me, it was obvious: "It depends, Sir. If the water is hot, then moving around will release steam and the water will cool; if the water is cold then moving around will create friction and heat it up." I enjoyed his classes, though he often poked fun at me. I was never particularly agile and in fact, slightly on the chubby side. One morning, he was behind me walking up the steps to the physics lab, and he said, "Come on, Linda, you are like a ten-ton lorry with a Mini engine!" Such a good quip for a physics teacher.

Despite everything, I worked hard at school, passed my GCE O-levels and, at 16, stayed on to take Advanced Level exams. I especially loved maths. I liked the certainty of it. There was always a right answer and, if you worked through the problem in a logical way, you would find it. It wasn't a discussion or a matter of opinion but was based on reasoning. From an early age I liked to count things; I'd count the cutlery, how many steps I walked, or stairs climbed. I looked for patterns in numbers, in shapes, on wallpaper. Like Mum, I enjoyed organising and sorting. I learned from Dad about angles and lines and taking accurate measurements. If I saw a crane, I'd try to understand why it could lift such heavy loads - weights, pulleys, levers.

Maths made sense to me, and it was all I wanted to do when the time came to choose A-Level subjects. I hated chemistry because it was so dry and dull; my friends would hear me repeat many times, "I don't care what I do at A level as long as it isn't chemistry." I chose maths, further maths and physics as my three main subjects to study for the two years leading up to university. Of course, 'choosing' and 'getting' are two different things. In the September that I was due to start A levels the further maths teacher left the school and no replacement could be found. The head teacher told me that, according to the timetable, the only other subject I could take was chemistry. I was devasted, disappointed, dreading more rote learning of the Periodic Table and the study of inorganic matter. I'm now sure that chemistry is a wonderful subject to study but, in 1966, it wasn't for me.

By the end of the first year, I was pretty fed up spending all my time on maths and physics and worrying that I wouldn't make the grade in chemistry. So aged 17 I decided to leave school and bring in a wage to help Mum out. I was quite pleased with myself at being offered a decently paid job in the laboratory of a prestigious cookware company.

My older sister had left home a few years earlier and moved to London to a job in the Civil Service which had good prospects and included her accommodation. Maybe I envied her the swinging sixties in London which hadn't quite reached Burnley. The local youth club was as far as I got, listening to the 60s sounds over and over: the Ronettes; the Crystals; Billy Fury; but that was about it.

Mum was disappointed when I told her about the job and said she would much rather I stayed at school. So, I did.

Little did I realise that my whole world was about to change.

Chapter 2 Hello Computer

"Come along and say hello to a computer" my maths teacher said one morning. It was 1967 and I wondered what had inspired her to say that. She was a nun, Sister Mary Philip, and it wasn't something I'd have expected her to say. Had she been watching Star Trek or Tomorrow's World on the TV? Was she serious?

"Who would like to come – I'm organising a trip to Manchester?" Hands shot up – yes please.

There were twelve of us in the A level maths class, so she arranged a minibus and a driver to take us on the 25-mile journey. On the way, I asked what had inspired her to take us to see a computer.

"You must see a computer before you leave school. I've heard our Prime Minister, Harold Wilson, talk about 'the white heat of technology', and he's right – it is the future. Besides, I've been reading about a wonderful woman in Chicago, the first woman to graduate with a PhD in Computer Science. What's more, she is a nun too, Sister Mary Kenneth Keller. I thought if she can work with computers why can't we - why can't you - my girls?"

I'd seen computers in movies: Batman with his 'Navigation Aid Computer' in the Batcave tracking the baddies around Gotham City; a ship controlled by a central computer in 'The Human Computer: Voyage to the Bottom of the Sea'. I could only imagine what they were capable of.

We headed for the John Dalton College of Technology in Manchester, opened by Harold Wilson only a year earlier. Sister Mary Philip's excitement was infectious.

My first computer – the Elliot 803 – 1967

As we entered the computer room, we saw five or six white cabinets, about three feet high, arranged in a row. On top of the cabinets were two grey heavy-looking metal machines with paper tape hanging out of them. In the middle was a console with lots of switches and flashing lights. We'd never seen anything like it before and were curious to find out what it could do.

Mr Brown, one of the college staff, explained: "Say hello to the Elliot 803 — it's a second-generation computer built using transistors instead of valves. It has 4K of core memory and a central processing unit housed in these cabinets."

"Hello computer!" we called out and laughed.

"What about the paper tape — what is that for?" I asked.

"The tape holds the program — the instructions you want to give to the computer — and the data you want as input to the program. This machine reads the paper tape and this one outputs the results onto paper tape."

"The paper tape has holes in it — how can you read it?" asked a classmate.

"Each row of holes represents a letter, number or other character in binary, noughts and ones, so that the computer can read it."

Fascinated, I asked, "Can you show us how it works?"

"Suppose we ask it to add two numbers together. First, we prepare the tape with the instructions and the data, and then feed it through the paper tape reader. What two numbers would you like?"

"87 and 965."

He prepared the tape and pressed some switches on the console to activate the tape reader. We could see the lights changing and then, in no time at all, paper tape was being printed out.

He fed the tape through a teletype and the number 1,052 was printed out.

"Is that correct?" he asked me. Regretting having chosen such a big number, I quickly did a mental calculation. "Yes," I said, excitedly. "Yes, it is correct."

Amazing! "Can I try it? Subtract two numbers maybe?" Mr Brown kindly showed me which instructions I needed to change and left me to it: use the teletype to create the paper tape, feed the tape into the computer, set some switches, take the tape from the output device, run it through the teletype to see the result. Eureka - I loved it.

I knew from that moment that I must find a way to work with computers.

1967 was an eventful year: I met my first computer and I met Patrick. It happened at Halloween, when a group of his friends and a group of my friends met to climb up Pendle Hill, famous for the witch trials of 1612, and the place to go on a dark All Hallows eve to hunt for witches. We met at Barley, walked partway up and then all decided to go back to one of our friend's house. It was too late to go home, so most of us just sat around talking and drinking until daylight. Patrick was lying under the hearthrug making up jokes and no-one, especially me, could sleep for laughing. I thought about him a lot after that and, although I was officially going out with his friend, it wasn't long before we got together.

Our first date didn't go too well. Every time I'd seen Patrick, he had been wearing blue jeans and a cowboy-style checked shirt, while I usually wore a sixties-style waisted dress and a cardigan or woollen coat. However, this time he'd decided to dress 'up' and arrived in a three-piece suit, a black overcoat and carrying a rolled umbrella. He said he wanted to take me to a nightclub but, when he saw how I was dressed, said he couldn't. I'd decided to dress 'down' to match his usual style and had turned up in purple flared pants and a brown two-tone jacket – far too casual to go to a nightclub. It went so badly I thought we'd never go out again.

Home wasn't conducive to studying, so I went to the library most nights after school. I worked on as many past exam papers as I could find and tried to get good grades. Not many working-class people went to university in the late 1960s and I knew that I was privileged to have the opportunity.

In 1966, there were only 40 universities in the UK, compared with almost 140 in 2017. In a bid to democratise education, university tuition fees were paid by the state and local authorities offered means-tested maintenance grants to help with living costs. [2] I was fortunate that applying to university was an option for me regardless of my family finances.

The first computer science undergraduate degree was launched in Manchester in 1965, but even Sister Mary Philips felt it safer to stick with maths. It was the foundation of most science subjects and would give me more career options. I applied to do maths and psychology at Manchester University, and pure and applied maths at Sheffield where they promised computing options in the second year.

Mum was really pleased when I was offered a place at Sheffield University. She applied for the means-tested maintenance grant from Lancashire County Council and was awarded the full amount. I've no idea how much it was, but I do remember being much better off at university than students from a middle-class background who received less maintenance. Their parents were supposed to top up the maintenance grant, but many didn't.

She bought me new clothes – I don't know how she managed to afford them. My favourites were an A-line Harris tweed cream-and-brown coat and knee-high brown patent-leather boots. She wanted me to feel confident because she knew I would be meeting people who were much better off than me. Many people at university were from wealthier families whose parents were doctors or lawyers and she wanted me to be self-confident, both in the way I looked as well as in the way I felt.

Actually, I did feel really confident, not in any way intimidated or shy. I knew I was good at my subject; I knew I was a strong person because I'd been through so much. I knew I was loved, so I'd every reason to be confident, and I did feel fabulous in my new clothes.

It turns out Patrick and I did meet again. I was excited to be going to university, a fresh start, a new challenge. At first, I thought I would leave Patrick behind in Burnley, but it wasn't to be, for by the end of the third week I was desperate to see him. He made the journey over by bus at the weekend (none of us had cars at that time) and I sneaked him into my room at the halls of residence. I was in an all-girls hall for first-year students and boys were strictly forbidden. The (female) warden would walk the corridors in the evening to check for any signs of the opposite sex. She was a tall, gaunt woman in her fifties, with short, permed hair, and below-the-knee tweed skirt. She often knocked at my door. I'd open it very slightly.

"Sorry to disturb you; I only have a pound note and need coins for the washing machine; do you have any?" she would say as she peered over my shoulder to see if anyone else was in the room.

I usually said, "No, sorry", and tried to shut the door, but she could be persistent.

"I only need two shillings; I'm sure you must have that in your purse". She just wanted me to move away from the door so could she peer in further.

We got wise to her tricks; I kept a supply of change near the door and at the first sound of her footsteps in the corridor Patrick would hide in the wardrobe. She got wise to our tricks too, and would stand quietly outside our door after we thought she'd left. If she heard us giggle or talk, she would knock again.

It was a 50-mile journey from Burnley to Sheffield. Communication was harder in 1968, with no mobile phones or text or the Internet. I wrote Patrick a letter every few days and he wrote back. His family did have a telephone in their living room, and I could ring him from a call box in the student halls, but it wasn't very private for either of us. I did miss him, and he missed me.

Before too long, Patrick moved over to Sheffield and got a job as a compositor in a printing firm. We shared a flat together, but our parents were not too happy about the arrangement, especially not his mum. She was older than my mum, having been born in 1902 and a staunch Catholic who thought it immoral for us to live together without being married. So, at the end of my second year, we got married. We didn't have much money and neither did our parents, but we had a lovely wedding at our local church and a reception at the Catholic Club. Friends and family mostly contributed in-kind instead of buying gifts: taking photographs, making the buffet, the wedding cake and a pie-and-pea supper. It was the eve of my twenty-first birthday.

Patrick had arranged a surprise honeymoon in Paris. It didn't sound so romantic at first since we were to travel all the way by coach. I'd never been abroad before and was excited to see the great French capital. We stayed in a low-cost hotel near Gare du Nord railway station and toured the city on foot. One evening, standing across the road from the Folies Bergère, Patrick said, "I've seen The Folies at the pictures – the dancing girls wear extravagant costumes and tall plumed headdresses". He was looking longingly at the large dancing figure above the doorway of the Alhambra-style building.

I joined him in his reverie: "I wish we could see them".

"Hey, you wanna see the Folies?" an American woman called from across the road.

"We'd love to, but …"

"Do you want these tickets?" her husband called out. "We bought them but have run out of time."

"Oh gosh! Thank you so much." We felt really special and fortunate. We got to see the Folies and had the best seats in the house.

We spent one blissful September week in Paris then returned to Sheffield. Patrick encouraged me in my studies at university. He was from a working-class background, similar to my own, and was proud of my achievement. None of his friends or family had been to university; at that time only 7% of the UK population went, and without financial support from the government I wouldn't have gone either.

Most of the first year at university was spent learning pure and applied maths, probability and statistics. Although I loved pure maths, one downside was that seminars were at 9 am on a Saturday morning, which meant I had to leave Patrick in my room while I went to class. Our tutor, Miss Perfect, really did seek perfection in all our work: she insisted on full attendance and completion of every exercise. She encouraged us to work together, and by the end of the first semester we were voluntarily researching pure maths topics and enjoying giving lunchtime talks to each other.

Scientific programming was an option in the second year, and I jumped at the chance to learn more about computers. I was excited to learn the programming language FORTRAN IV; its name is derived from 'Formula Translation' and was particularly suited to numeric computation. It was one of the languages being used in the Apollo Lunar missions 1968 - 1972, for example, to perform analysis of test-firing data, analysis of rocket combustion performance and spacecraft thermal analysis.

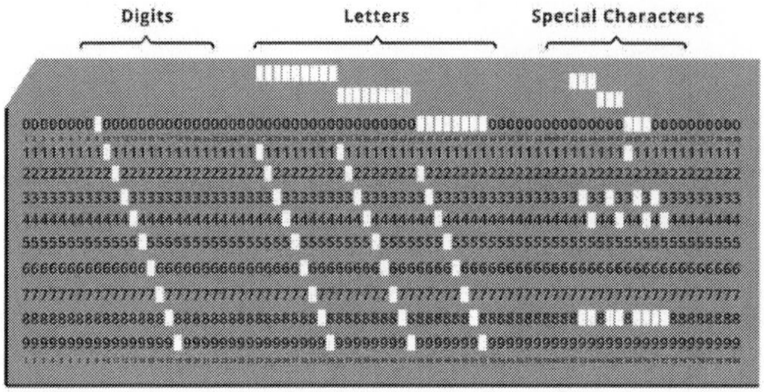

punched card – each column represents a number, letter or special character (%?<=>)*

We used punched cards when writing a FORTRAN program; one card represented one instruction, and we had a special machine to punch holes into the cards. A punched card is a piece of stiff paper that holds digital data represented by the presence or absence of holes in predefined positions. We used IBM cards which were 7.375in x 3.25in printed with a grid of 80 columns and 12 rows. A simple FORTRAN IV program that calculates the area of a triangle would need a minimum of 22 punched cards, one for each line of code[1]. Even a modest-sized program could result in a large box of cards and woe betide you if you dropped the box. Putting the cards back in the correct order could take hours.

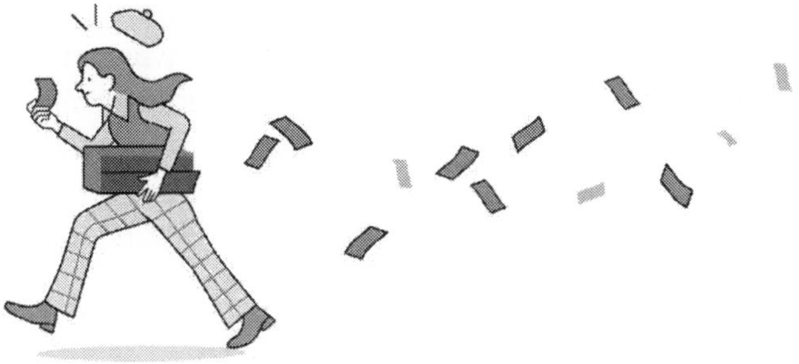

Despite the tedium of using punched cards, I gained a great deal of satisfaction from the process of submitting a stack of cards, waiting a day for them to be processed by the computer operators, collecting a print-out of the results, locating and correcting the errors and re-submitting until eventually I got the correct results. Finding and solving problems (i.e., debugging) is a big part of computer programming, and using punched cards was so tedious it made you super careful to test your program by hand before submission.

I enjoyed solving mathematical problems by computer but had only a cursory understanding of how the computer worked and was keen to find out more. By 1971 computer science was becoming a priority subject for the UK Science Research Council (SRC) and they offered a small number of bursaries for high-performing graduates to study for a master's degree. With the recommendation of my tutors, I won a bursary and a place at the University of St Andrews, Scotland, to study for a research

[1] See the Appendix for an example of a Fortran IV program that calculates the area of a triangle

master's in the Department of Computational Science. I was looking forward to it; in many ways Scotland seemed like home, with memories of childhood, my grandparents and the soft lilt of east coast accents. An October start gave us three months free.

We'd been saving up all year, having moved out of our self-contained flat with a garden into one grim room with shared kitchen and bathroom overlooking the cemetery. It was a good decision financially but not at all conducive to studying, and I spent most of my final year tense and stressed that I wouldn't make the grade.

Patrick gave up his job and, spurred on by our Parisian experience, we decided to travel further afield.

Chapter 3 Paging Algorithms

We planned to start our travels at Hellinikon airport in Greece[2]. It was the early 1970s and the hippie trail to India was at its height, but not everyone welcomed what appeared to be cash-strapped, unwashed dropouts in pursuit of nirvana. Rumours abounded that anyone looking like a hippie would be stopped at customs and turned back. Patrick fitted the picture with his long hair and long beard.

It would be the first time I'd ever been on an aeroplane, and I was anxious that our journey might end in the Athens airport, so I pleaded with him to get his hair cut. I went on and on, and eventually he did.

What a disaster! He came home from the hairdressers looking really upset, distraught, as if it wasn't him any longer and he didn't know who he was. What had I done? It didn't even suit him.

I was upset, he was upset, and I vowed I would never, ever nag him again.

Just let him be himself.

Much to my relief, no questions were asked at customs about Patrick's Irish name or his appearance. Feeling relieved and, with a sense of freedom, we headed straight for the islands. We didn't have a plan except to get to Istanbul, and then hitch a lift to India. We stopped off on the island of Tinos, calm, quiet and welcoming with beautiful blue skies, the Aegean Sea and white houses. We took a bus to the furthest point of the island and pitched our tent among some shady trees near the beach. Idyllic.

We discovered a small taverna and soon made it our regular spot for breakfast and evening meals. One day, after having eaten the most amazingly fresh eggs fried in olive oil and

[2] Hellinikon airport became Athens International Airport in 2001

sprinkled with freshly ground pepper, Patrick decided to walk a few yards to the low sea wall and lay down on it. He fell fast asleep, and his snoring attracted the attention of a group of young Greek boys, 8 or 10 years old. They stood around for a while, watching him with his beard moving up and down with the rhythm of his breathing (looking not unlike Ben Gunn from Treasure Island). The boys then went to the beach to collect pebbles which they duly started throwing at Patrick. This went on for quite a while, but he showed no signs of waking. The boys were having such fun.

I eventually shooed them off and woke Patrick. Apart from anything else he was at serious risk of getting sunburnt.

Just as it was becoming dark, we decided to go back to our two-man tent. Clearly, the boys hadn't had enough fun; they had put a goat inside the tent and zipped it up. The poor goat was bewildered, had made many attempts to get out and made a terrible mess everywhere; I can still smell it.

We stayed a little longer in Tinos and then headed by boat to the island of Samos, a lovely, unspoilt island with the advantage of only being one mile from Turkey. We had the idea of staying there for a few days and then taking the short boat ride across. Unfortunately, the Greeks and the Turks were not on friendly terms and the crossing by sea was closed.[3]

While we were enjoying the hospitality of Samos, a number of other travellers turned up also hoping to make the crossing: Canadians, South Africans and Australians. We decided to team up, making a group of eight, and raised enough money to persuade a local fisherman with a boat to take us across. It was a surprisingly rough crossing, and I spent the whole time hanging over the side of the boat being violently sick.

We landed at the small town of Kusadasi[4], where the boatman set us down and returned to Samos, not wishing to be seen. We decided to stay together as a group and managed to engage a driver and minibus to take us to Istanbul. We visited the ancient city of Ephesus to see the Temple of Artemis [5], and stopped at Izmir and a number of small towns en route.

We didn't see many women in the streets and those we did see were covered from head to foot in black. The driver advised the women in our group to cover arms and legs so as not to attract too much attention. Not everyone was willing to heed the advice and, one evening when we were having dinner in a taverna, our Canadian friend decided she would get up and dance to the music wearing only shorts and a rather tight T-shirt. I watched, mesmerised by her actions, then looked around and realised that the whole glass frontage of the café was covered with men's faces, eyes peering in, lots and lots of them vying for a position to view this dancing, abandoned western woman.

---

[3] There was a long history of hostilities between the two countries over territorial waters and the right to land. 1974 saw the Turkish Invasion of Cyprus.

[4] Kusadasi had a population of around 9,000 in 1970 rising to 50,000 by the year 2000.

[5] one of the Seven Wonders of the Ancient World.

I was worried for our safety on the walk back to our lodgings and didn't sleep well that night.

We eventually reached Istanbul[6]. It was so exotic; the streets and pavements were crowded and chaotic with sounds that were strange to me - the call to prayer from the mosques and the crowing of roosters from the rooftops. The sights were breath-taking, like nothing I had ever seen before: the huge Topkapi Palace with stunning blue-tiled rooms, the iconic Suleymaniye Mosque on the hill overlooking the city and the Grand Bazaar with hundreds of colourful shops in a bewildering network of streets where, despite being low on funds, I managed to barter for a beautiful Afghan coat to take home.

We did see offers of lifts to India in our hostel, but by this time we'd been away for twelve weeks and it was time to return home.

Except for the ferry crossing to England, we hitch-hiked all the way from Istanbul to Burnley. We were given a lift from Istanbul to Edessa in northern Greece by a very kind German who bought us lunch en route. We had several lifts to Dubrovnik, then to Split, working our way up the Yugoslavian[7] coast. Nearly everywhere we went in Yugoslavia, boys would run alongside us shouting the names of English footballers, such as Bobby Charlton, George Best and Nobby Stiles; it was their way of being friendly. Next, we travelled on to Munich in Germany, Brussels in Belgium, then took the ferry to England and finally headed north.

Exhausted, after travelling over two thousand miles, we briefly visited our respective families in Burnley to let them know that we were alive and well. They didn't seem too concerned; Patrick's mum even asked us to wait until her

[6] Istanbul had a population of 2million in 1970 rising to 15 million by 2015.

[7] What was Yugoslavia in 1971 is now Bosnia and Herzegovina, Croatia, Kosova, Montenegro, North Macedonia, Serbia and Slovenia.

favourite TV programme, 'Coronation Street', had finished before she got up to greet us.

The summer was over, and now my overriding objective was to travel to St Andrews and continue my education. I was keen to find out more about computers and how they worked.

Patrick quickly secured a job as a compositor at a printing company in Dundee; we found a place to rent in Tayport, mid-way between St Andrews and Dundee, and I was ready to start.

St Andrews was impressive: an ancient town with a cathedral dating back to medieval times and the university itself, the oldest in Scotland, founded in 1413. I loved the beautiful old stone and the feel of the breeze coming in from the sea. It often felt cold and on some days the mist would roll in from the sea. It would hang low on the ground and have the strange effect of making people invisible from the waist down, only their upper body visible above the mist.

Everyone was very friendly; hearing so many lovely Scottish accents reminded me of my childhood and I immediately felt at home.

The School of Computational Science was housed in a new building and its first degree in Computer Science had only recently been founded by Professor A. J. (Jack) Cole. I'm fairly sure that mine was the first cohort of research masters. We were a small group of six. I was the only woman, if a somewhat liberated one: I wore short skirts, black twenty-denier-seamed tights and knee-length boots, not your typical tweed skirt and woolly jumper of the serious female academic. After all it was 1972.

As a research master's student, I could choose my own research topic and decide which classes (if any) to attend. There were no exams, just a written dissertation at the end of 12 months.

I stuck with the idea of wanting to find out more about how the computer worked and my supervisor guided me towards time-sharing computers which were emerging as prominent models of computers at the time [3]. I understood a computer as consisting of three parts: 1. some kind of input; 2. a way of processing that input; and 3. some way of outputting the results.

Let me explain. In order to process the input, the computer needs some instructions – the program. Here is a simplified program to add two numbers:

```
INPUT A, B
C = A + B
OUTPUT C
```

If the data input gives A the value of 2 and B the value 3, then the number output will be 5.

If the data input gives A the value of 50 and B the value of 5 then the output will be 55.

And so on, for no matter which two numbers are input as data, the program will calculate their sum and output the result.

Both the input data and the program are stored in the physical memory of the computer and my experience so far was of computers that could only process one job (program) at once. The input data and the program were punched onto punch cards, fed into the computer and then the results printed out on paper. Each new job had to wait in the queue for the previous one to finish.

The idea of storing both data and program was referred to as the stored-program computer and first became operational as long ago as 1948 when the Manchester 'baby machine' was created.[8] These first-generation computers used vacuum tubes.

Even though it was rather large, the Manchester computer was too slow to perform realistic calculations, and it wasn't until

[8] A working model of the Manchester 'baby' is on permanent display at Manchester Museum of Science and Industry, https://www.scienceandindustrymuseum.org.uk/whats-on/meet-baby Accessed 30/01/22

1949 that Cambridge University completed the 'EDSAC', a first-generation computer and the first full-scale stored-program computer to go into regular service.

Ten years later IBM brought out the IBM 1401 computer that used transistors instead of electronic tubes and paved the way for faster, more reliable machines [4].

Powerful as these computers were, they could only process one job at once. If programmers wanted to test their programs, they had to book the computer out, say for an hour, have sole use of it, and then give it up for the next person. If the programmer hadn't completed their work, they had to go to the end of the queue to wait for another one-hour time slot.

Throughout the 1960s there were many attempts to solve this problem by exploring the idea of time-sharing, that is, allowing more than one program to run at once thus speeding up the processing of jobs. Time-sharing was still a topic of much debate when I came to do my master's degree and as such, an interesting subject for research. What's more, it was an ideal subject to help with my personal development as it necessitated a much deeper understanding of what happens within the computer itself. The basic idea was to alter the way that the computer allocated time and memory space so that it could handle several jobs at the same time, achieving this by allowing each job only a small amount of processing time before going on to the next job and by using an external memory (at that time, magnetic discs) to store programs or segments of programs temporarily until they were needed again. In essence, my master's degree was about developing and testing algorithms for managing both the amount of processor time allocated to each job and the swapping of the programs and segments in and out external memory as required. These were called 'paging algorithms' and helped create what was referred to as 'virtual memory' [3].

It wasn't practical to test my paging algorithms on an actual computer because I would need to have sole use of the departmental computer for a considerable time and neither staff nor students would be very happy about that. Therefore, I had to build a simulator [5] that would behave like a computer.

I built the simulator in FORTRAN on an IBM 360/44 in the computer laboratory of the Department of Computational Science, and I used performance data from the Manchester ATLAS computer for testing the validity of the simulator.

I developed three different paging algorithms and ran them through the simulator to assess the effectiveness of each one in terms of speed of processing jobs and efficient use of both processor and memory. The algorithms were designed to avoid the problem of 'thrashing', which can occur if there is too much swapping between external and core memory, so much swapping, in fact, that no jobs get completed.

The simulator worked well, and I was encouraged to develop it into a teaching tool for undergrads to learn about time-sharing and paging algorithms.

The final challenge was to type up my dissertation. I wrote it by hand, but it had to be typed up before submission and, with only a manual typewriter, this was proving very difficult. There were too many typos, too many restarts, it was incredibly frustrating and I couldn't type anyway. When the departmental secretary offered to type it for me on her newly acquired electric typewriter, I was truly grateful. She managed to do all the text and leave gaps for me to insert mathematical formulas and diagrams by hand. It took almost a year after finishing the research to actually produce a typed, bound dissertation. None of this seemed to bother the department; no doubt everyone had the same problem.

St Andrews was a happy experience, with beautiful historic surroundings and world-class scholars and tuition.

People were warm and friendly towards me and I met students from backgrounds quite different from my own.

It may sound odd, but one incident in particular sticks in my mind. We were invited to dinner at a fellow student's house; he and his girlfriend were still preparing the food when we arrived. My offer of help was declined, but I did stay in the kitchen long enough to witness them chopping an onion. Neither of them had any idea what to do. First, they carefully took the brown outer skin off and peeled off the first layer of onion flesh; then, realising that there were lots of layers, they began to remove them one by one, trying to keep the shape intact. Having got a chopping board covered with a dozen or so ball-shaped onion layers, they proceeded to chop each one. This all took an incredible amount of time, but they seemed really pleased with themselves. How could they not know how to chop an onion? Their upbringing was clearly quite different to mine.

I had thoroughly enjoyed the masters and had a better understanding of the internal workings of the computer and of the relationship between the external disk memory and the internal core memory. I was offered the opportunity to stay on for another two years and extend my research for a doctorate. However as much as I had enjoyed being a research student, I felt it was time to do something more applied and, of course, earn some money.

Professor Cole drew my attention to a potential job as an applications programmer. He had been contacted by a professor of pharmacology at Maryfield Hospital in Dundee who was looking for a suitable candidate for a new ward-based computer project.

I applied for the job on his recommendation and was invited for interview.

Chapter 4 Does your husband expect . . .

Autumn 1973, Maryfield Hospital, Dundee, Scotland - my first job interview. The role is Applications Programmer.

My new suit, with black-and-white jacket and knee-length skirt, makes me feel happy and I have a big smile on my face as I enter the interview room. I feel confident in my technical ability and am ready to answer any questions.

"Good morning, Mrs Macaulay; come in, please sit here." The chairman shows me to a seat at one end of a large oval table and the sight of five middle-aged men at the other.

He introduces the panel: council officers, administrators from Tayside Health Board and a city councillor. No-one technical, no one from the project I would be working on — my confidence wanes — what on earth will they ask?

They look at me, then look at my application, then back at me. What are they thinking —a young woman — how unusual — can she really do this job? The questioning begins.

The chairman, a red-headed Scot proudly sporting a green tartan tie, his clan tartan perhaps, is in control, though he appears a little nervous repeatedly touching his tie and shirt cuffs.

"We just want to check a few points from your application. You recently graduated from St. Andrews?" I'm thinking that's a plus point – they are familiar with the university.

"Yes, from the School of Computational Science."

"You worked with Professor A J Cole?" he enquired, showing that he had read the application, or maybe he was impressed because Prof Cole was well-known.

"Yes, I studied for a master's degree in his research group."

Next, the Councillor, a bald, rotund man in a grey suit speaks

"You've applied for a job as an applications programmer. What exactly is an applications programmer?"

Surely, he knows what the job is, but perhaps not. I thought I'd better explain.

"It is a person who writes instructions that enable people to use the computer to do their job. An example would be instructions that enable a nurse to record information about a patient." He seems happy with that.

Next, I hear a strong Dundee accent coming from the council officer.

"Does your husband expect his tea on the table when he gets in from work?"

What did he say? I ask him to repeat the question. Why are they asking me about my husband? This is the 1970s, I'm 23 and I'm hardly likely to sit at home worrying about his tea. I decide an honest reply is best.

"Well, he might expect his tea on the table, but whether he gets it or not is another matter."

They all laugh.

The chairman kindly explained that as I would be working in a hospital, I may need to work odd hours and not always get home in time to make my husband's tea. They just wanted to make sure that wasn't a problem.

I thought maybe they should interview my husband.

They were struggling for relevant questions to ask and I felt that, if I'd been a male candidate, they would probably have asked me about golf or cricket.

Nonetheless, I was very pleased when they offered me the job.

Maryfield, an old-fashioned Victorian hospital from the 1890s, was in the throes of closing down. My appointment was to be at the brand new Ninewells Hospital.

Patrick and I were now both working in Dundee, so we decided to move to Newport-on-Tay, a lovely small town on the River Tay and an easy bus ride across the road bridge into Dundee. Our flat was tiny, more like a caravan for size but with an amazing view across the mile-wide river.

On my first day at work, I discovered that we were to be a team of three: Norrie, the Project Manager, Richard, the System Designer and myself the Applications Programmer. We were all newly appointed. The Professor of Pharmacology, Prof James Duncan was our boss, the one who had funding for the project and the one with the vision, and who knew what he wanted, (or so we thought).

Prof Duncan was a tall, imposing man with a ruddy face, bushy eyebrows and the soft lilt of an Edinburgh accent. There was a slight smell of cigars in the room which made me imagine him in his wax jacket and plus fours ready for a grouse-shooting trip in the Highlands.

We all sat on easy chairs on the opposite side of the room to his desk; he tried to be relaxed and informal but that wasn't really his style. He was a scientist, a busy man and wanted to get on with the task in hand.

The project was called 'The Ward Based Computer System'. In the UK, in the early 70s, there was no such thing, everything was paper-based, and computers were too big and noisy to sit on hospital wards. This pioneering work was funded directly by the Medical Research Council.

The three of us met the professor each week to find out what he had in mind, and each week he would tell us something different. At first, we thought we didn't understand, because he was a medical man, after all, and we were computer people.

Norrie conscientiously wrote down everything the professor had asked for. It felt like enough for a lifetime's work. It is impossible to write a computer program without a specification of what it is supposed to do: inputs, processes, outputs. Among the three of us, we decided that we should pick a couple of ideas, design and program them, then see if they would work on a ward and seek feedback from the doctors and nurses. Meanwhile, Norrie would continue the meetings with Prof Duncan, and Richard and I would embark on building something. We'd come across some inspirational work in the US [6] and decided to start with the daily nursing schedules and the doctors' ward round.

Great. We had started. There was only one problem - the computer.

The Professor's choice of computer was directly influenced by the government's strategy that the NHS should 'buy British', and he had bought it before we arrived. The CTL Modular One, a 16-bit minicomputer, was designed to be 'modular', resulting in almost every system being different. This meant that the processor, memory, magnetic disk drives and peripherals were delivered as separate cabinets and were not yet connected. We were rather taken aback, none of us having built a computer before. Together we unpacked the boxes, put the cabinets in place and then it was up to me.

The first part of the task was to connect the various parts of the computer and get them to communicate with each other, then to install the disk operating system and finally configure it to interact with the core memory.

I used a low-level programming language, called Assembler, that corresponded more closely to the computer's own machine code than other languages I knew. Still, there was a manual!

Program instructions were typed into the teletype which converted them into punched paper tape. The tape was then removed from the teletype and fed into the paper tape reader on the computer. All output was via a printer. It was a slow process.

The minicomputer occupied a room approximately 7 metres by 5 metres and at times became very hot. The air was dry and there was a problem with static; every time I operated the paper tape reader or touched something metal, I got a shock. It was worse in winter, when I used to get a tingling sensation in my legs. In time, I realised it was because I was wearing two pairs of tights. Dundee had a lot of clear, crisp winter days, but they were very cold, and I would wear two pairs of thick tights to keep me warm on the journey to work. The static would find its way between the tights and have me hopping around. I tried boiling a kettle to generate steam and create damp air; this worked for a while but was not a particularly safe option. The room was in a part of the hospital not yet fully operational; it still looked like a building site from the windows, with the grounds not yet landscaped.

If it wasn't too cold, I would open the windows to cool the room. One Monday morning, I came in and found they'd been open all weekend. I could not get the computer to work; I tried everything I could think of and then decided to take the backs off the cabinets to see if any wires were disconnected. What a sight: earwigs everywhere, crawling all over the cables, snuggling in the crevices.

We really did have computer bugs!

No doubt they came in to get warm over the weekend. I picked the soft squishy things off the cables one by one, threw them back outside and closed the windows. I developed a dislike for earwigs with their thin bodies, pincers and skin wings, and prayed they wouldn't come back.

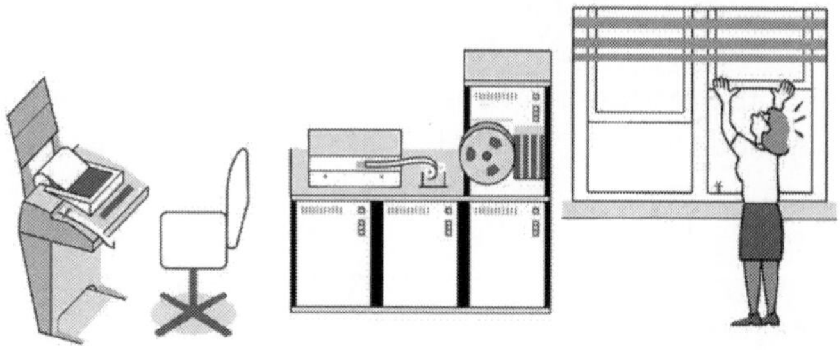

CTL Modular One and teletype – 1973

I wasn't the first programmer to discover bugs in the computer – as long ago as 1947 the pioneer Grace Hopper[9] recorded that a moth stuck between relay contacts in the Harvard Mark II had caused a computer failure. She coined the term 'computer bug' which is now commonplace and refers to an error or fault in a computer program or a hardware system, 'debugging' being the process of identifying and removing errors.

[9] Grace Hopper (1906-1992) was an American Computer Scientist, a United States Navy rear admiral and a pioneer of computer programming. The Harvard Mark II was an electromechanical computer built for the United States Navy.

With the bugs gone, and the computer all connected up and working, we were ready to do some applications programming. I spent most of my time in the computer room on my own, writing programs and operating the computer. I quite enjoyed the rhythms of the machines, and I could usually tell if something was going wrong just by listening.

We used the real-time programming language Coral 66[10] which would enable us to produce applications that doctors and nurses could interact with directly. They could input data and expect a result quickly enough to be of practical use to them. [7]

We decided to start with the nurses' daily schedule, which typically included basic hygiene for patients: bathing, clothing, changing bed linen; administering medication; maintaining patients' charts and recording assessment data, such as blood pressure and temperature.

Prior to writing any computer programs, we had to be able to specify in more detail what exactly nurses did in terms of workflow and use of data. Richard had some experience of systems analysis, which we conducted in two stages. First, fact-finding: interviews, questionnaires and visual observations of nurses at work. Second, gauging how users would operate the computer system, their experience of using computers, what the system would be used for and how it would fit into their everyday work.

I conducted interviews with nurses, and it was clear that while I was able to find out and record what they did, they had no idea what we were doing nor any knowledge of computers. Hardly surprising, as even the BBC's CEEFAX teletext service didn't start until 1974 – the general public's first experience of information retrieval, albeit on the television, using a three-digit number, for example 100 for news, 400 for weather. As a result, we decided that the only way for the nurses to learn about

---

[10] CORAL (Computer On-line Real-time Applications Language) CORAL 66 is a derivative of ALGOL and its definition first published in 1970

computers was for them to actually try using one. We trundled a teletype up to the ward; it was a monster at 35Kg and, being electromechanical, was very noisy. It was soon moved to a side room where nurses and some curious doctors would come in to try it out.

I wrote a program that output questions to the teletype and received replies from the user, i.e. an interactive dialogue. The teletype had no capacity for pictures, so everything was text. A question would be printed on the teletype paper and the nurse would answer via the keyboard. Unfortunately, each key took quite a bit of effort to press down, so even the shortest answer seemed to take ages, resulting in the feeling that the whole dialogue was being conducted in slow motion.

I was familiar with the Scottish accent and was surprised when one of the doctors said to me, "Linda, you realise you've written this in a Lancashire accent!"

This was an amusing quip, but then I realised that the phrasing and rhythm of my written sentences were akin to the way I spoke. I was writing in dialect. Should I feign a Scottish dialect, or ask the doctor to rephrase everything for me?

The experience taught me how easy it was to embody the subtleties of language into the computer program, the programmer assuming that everyone will understand it when in fact they may not.

I learned a great deal from the 'Ward Based Computer Project'. Firstly, as a programmer there's an assumption that people will tell you what they want you to program, and you just have to get on with it. This is far from the truth. People don't know exactly what they want. They express themselves in vague terms, are unsure, and have little understanding of what the computer is capable of doing. Secondly, even if they could tell you precisely what they want, no-one can predict the impact that the new system would have on the people who are expected to actually use it. Will they have the skills to operate it, how will it change their everyday job, will it improve things or make it worse? After all, nursing ward schedules and doctors' ward rounds are based on traditions that have evolved over many years.

Finally, when you write a computer program you are creating some future unknowable situation, because as soon as the computer is introduced into the nurses' working day their routine will change, procedures will change and interaction with each other and with patients will change. However, it is impossible to predict exactly how.

I learned that programming was the easy part; discovering the requirements and designing a system that was useful and usable was much more difficult.

It was a kind of eureka moment – no matter how good my technical expertise was, the resulting system wouldn't be effective if the interaction between the humans and the computer was ignored.

Difficult, but enjoyable, and so much more to learn.

Patrick was also enjoying his job but, one night, he said he was ready for a change and wanted to go travelling again. I'm not quite sure why he thought this; he'd been in his job longer than me so maybe he just felt trapped by the routine or since I'd had an early miscarriage that had perhaps set him thinking that we should travel again before a baby came along. We weren't trying for a baby, nor were we taking precautions, but just letting nature take its course.

What should I do, I'd been in my job only 18 months? I didn't really want to leave.

Employment levels were high, both our professions were in demand, so we could easily get a job on our return. It was agreed. We both handed in our notice on the same day and decided to head for Morocco, as we'd heard so much about it and loved its colours and textiles.

Within a week, we had a twelve-month British Visitor's Passport from the Dundee Employment Exchange. I was included on Patrick's passport as his wife, and as such was not allowed to travel unaccompanied by him. The passport was 'for British Subjects: Citizens of United Kingdom and Colonies[11] only' and with text in both French and English.

We had survived our earlier travels so, despite Patrick's hippie appearance, I no longer worried about his being stopped at customs.

We took the bus to London, then to Dover, crossed the channel by hovercraft to Calais and then hitch-hiked to Paris and through France into Spain. We had an idea to head for southern Spain in the hope of being able to cross to Algiers, travel along the northern coast of Africa to Tunisia and then take a boat to the toe of Italy and travel back.

Patrick's mother was unwell before we set off on our journey and he telephoned regularly to check on her health. We'd been away eight weeks, but only just reached southern Spain when he learnt that she was getting worse and that it might be prudent to return home.

Our best option was to take the train to San Sebastian in northern Spain. We wondered why everyone was carrying baskets of food, thinking the journey would take about 4 hours (it was 370 miles) and there would be a buffet car on board. How naive. It took 15 hours, and you could only get refreshments if you ran off the train at a station and grabbed something from a local vendor.

The baskets revealed whole roast chickens, loaves of bread, oranges, water and wine. Everyone was so kind; they laughed at our naivety and happily shared what they could. I had never tasted such delicious oranges.

Our travels were over.

---

[11] Colonies were territories ruled or administered by the United Kingdom and part of the British Empire.

Patrick's mum's health was worsening; it was cancer, and the prognosis was not good. We felt we should stay with her.

While we were travelling, I hadn't really noticed that I was three months pregnant. We talked it through, and it made sense for me to stay at home with his mum and for Patrick to find work.

Patrick's family all lived in the neighbourhood where they were raised and were very much part of the local community and church. When I went to the shops, I was greeted, "Ah, you're the new Mrs Macaulay." "Was I?" I thought "am I to become Patrick's mother?" We were living in her house and had decided to buy it from Patrick's older brother Denis. His other brother, John, still lived there - kind of included with the fixtures and fittings!

I found myself cooking meals for Patrick's mum, ourselves and John. He just wanted 'traditional' food: pie and chips, whilst his mum was on a fish-and-milk diet, and we were vegetarians, so every day was a culinary challenge. I drew the line at doing his brother's washing.

I went to the local shops every day, did the cooking, washing and cleaning, and managed as best I could with the £30 per week that Patrick earned. It was a reasonable wage for the time, but we had to count every penny. I kept a notebook listing spending and saved weekly for incoming bills and purchases such as a new vacuum cleaner. We didn't use credit, our only debt being the mortgage on the house.

Was this to be my new life?

As his mum's health deteriorated, Patrick, Denis and John took turns to sit with her during the night and his sister, Eileen, and I looked after her during the day. She didn't want to be in hospital and was happy to be surrounded by her loving family. She'd had a hard life and, like my own mother, was widowed with four young children to raise on her own.

She was kind, fun and a joy to look after.

As the weeks passed, she became weaker and thinner and spent much of the time sleeping. She spoke kindly when she was awake but gradually this was less and less.

She left us late one evening, with her children nearby. Her doctor, who had a young family of her own, was unable to come out at night and asked if we could wash her and lay her out until the morning.

Patrick's sister and I were happy to carry out this final act of love; we were gentle with her, caressing her frail body while cleansing and dressing it and laying her on the bed for the last time.

I was seven months pregnant.

Her precious life had gone from us, but new life was on its way.

Chapter 5 The computer revolution hits home

A Valentine's Day gift, a beautiful baby son born just two months after Patrick's mother passed away. What a joy to hold precious new life, a healthy, contented child christened Jon-Sebastian. He was our baby born from love and to be loved forever.

We always said we should take an equal share in bringing up children, ideally, by both working part-time or maybe taking turns, each staying three years at home followed by three years at work.

Before the baby was born, I had felt so strongly about sharing responsibility that I responded to an article in the local newspaper and a journalist interviewed me to obtain a fuller picture of my views. The half-page article appeared in the Burnley Express and News on 13th September 1974, titled 'WORK IT OUT' in capital letters. Under the heading 'TRAPPED' I was quoted:

"In most jobs today, women get equal pay; women have equal education, so why is the job of home-making not done on equal terms with men? Why are men trapped into working ... and why are women trapped at home? Surely there has to be a better solution to the way we live our lives. Why not make marriage a partnership at all levels and live on equal terms with each other?"

The journalist commented: "Not all women are as well-qualified as Linda to earn a man-sized salary . . . Many women earn low wages doing unskilled jobs and men are paid, on average, just about twice as much as women on a nationwide basis.

. . . men are conditioned from birth into accepting the role of breadwinner, shunning the idea of doing household chores which they have been taught to consider women's work.... And there are still a lot of men around who think like this ..."

It was 1975 and I expected attitudes to have changed. It was still largely assumed that women would stay at home once the baby was born, with maternity leave only six weeks and paternity leave not even heard of.

We both wanted to play a full role in bringing up our son and to make our own decisions about how we organised our lives. We both had good jobs, after all.

Or so we thought.

Patrick was a compositor, a craftsman who had served a five-year apprenticeship to learn his trade. He assembled a line of hot-metal type[12] onto a setting stick and then built up a page ready for printing on a letterpress machine or on a plate-making machine for lithographic printing. Shortly before the baby was born, his employer introduced a computer-phototypesetter system requiring only keyboard skills and direct data entry to set up pages ready for print. Patrick was asked to retrain as a typist.

The computer revolution had hit home; Patrick's skill and expertise were taken over by computer, a classic case of computers being used to de-skill jobs. While I had been busy computerising other people's jobs, my husband's role in the printing industry was itself being computerised.

Still keen to learn more about computers and an avid follower of the job market in Computer Weekly[13] it wasn't long before I saw a position I thought would suit me: a System Designer for the 'Three Labs Project' at The London Hospital, Hammersmith Hospital and Poole General Hospital. I could do everything on the tick list and had experience in the health service. I was aged 25.

I was invited for interview in London. A young man, aged 23, was waiting to be interviewed for a Project Manager's job, a position with more pay and a higher status than the one I was

[12] Hot-metal type is individual metal letters, numbers and other characters made from hot metal using a Linotype Machine.

[13] Computer Weekly, a UK newspaper from 1960 to 2010 now online https://www.computerweekly.com accessed 10/05/2021

applying for. I couldn't resist asking him questions: Have you worked as a project manager before? Answer: no. Is your degree in Management? Answer: no. Have you worked on health service projects before? Answer: no.

I couldn't believe it; he was very confident but ticked hardly any of the job description boxes. Why didn't I do that? I was sure if he could do the job then so could I. Did I lack confidence? I wrongly assumed that you had to prove that you could do the job before you got it. In my own interview it was clear that I knew more than anyone on the interview panel about the computers they were proposing to use.

The young man was hired for the Project Manager's job, and they offered me the position of System Designer; fortunately, we were not on the same team.

To be honest, I didn't want to be a project manager, preferring a more technical role, but I would welcome more pay and status.

My position was based in Poole General Hospital with occasional visits to The London Hospital. I went ahead to Poole to find a house and Patrick, now a stay-at-home Dad, and baby Jon followed. Poole is a coastal town in southern England with a large natural harbour and sandy beaches. The sale of our terraced house in Burnley and my salary were enough to buy a maisonette with a garden and a distant view of the sea. The transition wasn't easy, staying at my sisters in London and in temporary accommodation in Boscombe while the sale went through, but once settled we loved our new home.

The hospital itself was new, opened only six years earlier by Queen Elizabeth II. As a small team of three our task was to work with the Pathology Lab, and to convert the readings from their various machines into standard units. I had no idea there were so many bodily fluids and for each fluid a different machine was used for analysis, producing graphs, charts and numbers in different units of measurement. The problem from the doctors' point of view was that in order to assess the health of a particular patient they had to work through numerous paper-based results. Clearly, the computer couldn't directly read the paper results from the various machines, so these had to be converted into digital format. At the same time there was a national move to have all readings converted to Standard Units[14]. The overall goal was to produce one report for the doctors which contained results from all the readings: one report for one patient, all in Standard Units.

From a technical programming point of view, the project was relatively straightforward. The difficulty came with the realisation that the reports produced would be used by doctors to make decisions about the patients' treatments. This felt pretty scary. What if we got it wrong? What if the conversion to standard units was out by a decimal place? What if a glucose level was showing as high when in fact it was low or vice versa? Or the count of red blood cells was showing as low when in fact it was high?

If the reading on the results sheet was wrong and the doctors prescribed treatment accordingly, a patient could die or at least have adverse reactions. In which case whose fault was that? The doctors'? The programmers'?

The mathematical accuracy of the conversion was critical, and I made sure that my programs were tested and re-tested before releasing them anywhere near the labs.

Testing was great fun because it meant I had two screens running in real time showing me exactly what was happening inside the computer memory. I could detect bugs and fix them

---

[14] Standard Units are seven basic units of measurement accepted throughout the scientific world the meter (m), the kilogram (kg), the second (s), the kelvin (K), the ampere (A), the mole (mol), and the candela (cd).

as they occurred and really felt in control. The CTL Modular One had three internal registers: on one screen you could see the X Register which contained your program instructions and on a second screen you could see the Y register and the data output as each line of the program executed. Thus, I could follow the program step by step and check for errors and, even better, I could correct them as it went along.
All three of us on the project were competent programmers. The project manager divided the work between us. He didn't approve of my fun, interactive way of debugging programs preferring instead to do 'desk-checking': essentially this involved sitting at your desk going through every line of code by hand and writing down the outputs as you went along.

The CTL Modular One with two monitors – 1975

He was meticulous and would sit for hours desk-checking his program by hand before actually entering it into the computer. The most annoying part, from my point of view, was that his programs always worked first time!

Even more annoying, he would walk around the computer room and gloat, leaning over my shoulder to see where I was up to. "Haven't you finished yet, Linda?" In fact, he was a bit creepy with his jam-jar glasses, brown crumpled suit and a tendency always to look down. I had the feeling he was looking at my bosom; he never looked me (or anyone else) in the eye. Maybe he was shy. He would keep turning up somewhere in the near distance when Patrick and I were out at the weekend; I once saw him walking in front of our house, which was odd because we lived in a cul-de-sac.

The other member of our team was an enthusiastic Morris dancer, and he would tell me about the history and origins of the tradition, the details of the dress and the meaning of each dance. He was a nice guy but preoccupied and difficult to connect with.

Some days I would wander into the offices next door in search of female company. I didn't do too well because they couldn't relate to me at all, owing not only to the job I was doing but also to the fact that I had a child. "How could you leave your five-month-old baby?" "A baby needs its mother." Were they trying to make me feel guilty? I explained that the child had two parents and as long as one of them was looking after him then that was fine. "My husband loves his son, enjoys playing with him, teaching him and seeing him grow. That's lovely isn't it?"

Patrick would walk Jon-Sebastian down to Poole Park at lunchtime and we would sit and have a picnic lunch together. 1976 was a particularly warm year and our meetings, even in the winter, were the highlight of my day!

My work on this project coincided with a wider debate on the responsibilities of programmers. I had experienced some alarm when confronted with the idea that someone could actually die or be wrongly treated as a result of my errors. I became interested in the British Computer Society and their Code of Conduct[15] which actively sought to encourage a sense

---

[15] BCS Code of Conduct first published in 1972.
https://www.bcs.org/media/2211/bcs-code-of-conduct.pdf
Accessed 30/01/22

of professionalism among programmers and other computer staff.

Programming was relatively new and there was wider concern about the 'unmanageability' of programmers. Some branded programmers as 'prima donnas' who were 'arrogant', 'egocentric', and 'devoid of social skills'. There was a move to redefine 'programming' as 'software engineering' in the hope that it would instil the disciplines of engineering and make programmers more manageable. Unfortunately, 'engineering' at that time didn't have a great record for including women. Reporting on a personal interview Abbate [8] relates that even the IBM award-winning creator of an Advanced Compiler System, Fran Allen, received a physical prize of cufflinks and a tie-clip. Clearly, they hadn't thought that such an award could possibly go to a woman.

I was feeling somewhat confused at this stage. Professionally, I felt that we lacked the appropriate tools to do the job, particularly in the safety-critical environment of a hospital. Though collecting as much test data as possible and ensuring the mathematical accuracy of results, we couldn't prove that our programs would work in every case.

On a personal level, I felt that I didn't fit in; neither the man-geeks in the computer room nor the women in the offices offered any connection points. The wider computing profession was struggling with the inclusion of women (with a few notable exceptions [9]) and, although I had no doubts that I would continue with my passion, I felt it was going to be an uphill struggle.

Chapter 6 Microprocessors

Ready for my next move, I started to look for a new job. Excited to learn more about microprocessors and how they could be used, I was attracted to a post that I saw in Computer Weekly for a Lecturer in Computer Studies to teach computing to businesspeople and to explore the use of microprocessors with the local industry.

The microprocessor, Intel 4004, housed all the main computer components (the central processing unit, memory and input/output controls) onto a single black plastic casing. What filled a room in the 1960s would now fit in the palm of your hand. By 1976 the Intel 4004 had been on the market for almost five years but for many companies in the north of England the microprocessor revolution was only just beginning.

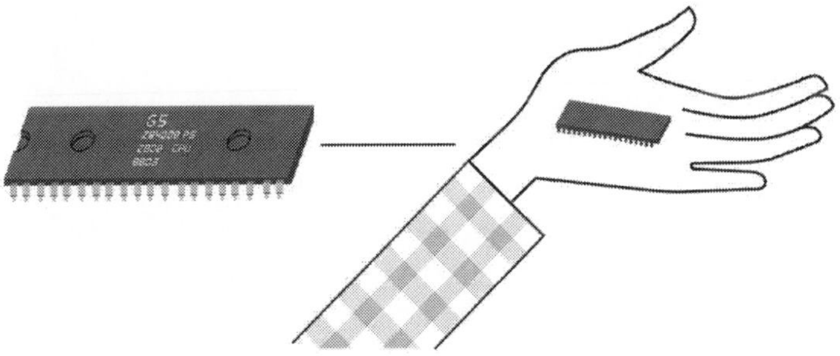

The revolutionary small microprocessor – 1976

By the mid-70s, microprocessors were being used in manufacturing to control processes and machines and, though I didn't know at the time, they would underpin the development of the personal computer and ultimately the connectivity of the Internet. This was the beginning of fourth-generation computers.

I was invited for an interview which went well and was offered the job. We were soon on our way back "up North", this time not to Lancashire, but Yorkshire, as my new post was at the Percival Whitley College in Halifax.

We bought a house on the outskirts of Halifax in the village of Akroydon, a Victorian model village built in 1860 by Colonel Edward Akroyd, a mill owner and philanthropist. The village is an arrangement of 90 houses around a square park with a Victoria Cross monument in the centre. Ours was a large five-bedroom house with two sitting rooms, two large basement rooms and a garden leading down to the park. The back bedrooms had lovely views of the hills, while those at the front faced a tree-lined street with a row of terraced houses opposite.

Halifax and the surrounding area, though known more widely for its woollen mills, had a growing number of companies making components for the manufacturing supply chain. At the time they would set up a machine to cut a sheet of metal to a particular design, either manually or using a prefabricated pattern guide. These processes were already numerically based, and computer numerical control was the logical next step.

Visiting manufacturing companies in 1978 was much grimmer than I had imagined. The factories were dark and grey. Men in grey overalls stood beside machines watching them and checking that the small metal components fell into large buckets, and others wheeled the buckets to another part of the factory floor. The men looked washed out, as if they lacked sunlight, and walked around like automata.

Typically, a manager would show me around, explaining as we went, then show me to an area on the factory floor where there was a table and half a dozen chairs. There might be a woman at the reception desk when I first arrived but there was no other woman in sight. At 27 years old I felt very young, a little self-conscious and not sure how I was going to connect with the factory management and union officials who were to occupy the seats. I'd worked out that there was usually at least one person who was keen to hear about the new technology and who acted as advocate for my being there. There was also at least one who was hostile and who asked questions outside my remit.

Standing at the desk, I would take out a few microprocessors and hand them round. The first thing to impress upon them was how small they were. Of course, in the late 1970s, not many people had seen a computer of any kind except on the television: 'Dr Who'[16] or 'Tomorrow's World'[17].

Next, I would try to explain how a microprocessor worked, that the black plastic casing contained a computer and that the pins were for connecting to other devices. I talked about the numeric instructions they currently gave to their cutting machines and explained that these could be converted to a computer program for automatic entry via the microprocessor to the machine, thus saving the time of the machine tool operator.

I didn't want to be too detailed in the technical explanation or to get over-excited about the possibilities. Enthusiastic as I was myself, I could see a look of disbelief on some faces, a worried look on others, as they absorbed what it would mean for jobs and the factory itself. Everyone was very polite towards me, after all I had been invited in by management, but sometimes I left feeling as if I had dropped a bomb in their midst.

They knew they had to embrace this revolutionary technology or be left behind. Visiting about a dozen factories around the area, I learned a great deal about people and the

---

[16] Doctor Who is a British science fiction television programme produced by the BBC since 1963.

[17] A popular BBC TV Programme about the latest trends in science & technology ran from 1965 for 38 years.

implications of technology for their working lives. I was also able to meet businesspeople at the evening classes at the college where we taught 'Introduction to Computers' and 'O' level and 'A' level Computer Studies. These mature students were interesting to teach because they always had stories to tell about their work that added to my own education.

Teaching evening classes was convenient for us. Patrick had been accepted as a mature student on a full-time foundation art course at the same college. We all travelled to college together in the mornings: Jon attended the creche, I worked until lunchtime and then took him home for the afternoon until Patrick came home for tea, when I returned to college for an evening class. I worked five mornings and three evenings. On the whole, it was a good arrangement for everyone; we didn't have a car and neither of us could drive, so we walked and pushed the pram up and down the Halifax hills.

At that time we were aware that the Yorkshire Ripper[18] was still at large in West Yorkshire. A few years earlier, in 1975, he had struck a woman (Olive Smelt) on the head several times with a hammer and left her for dead. She had lived only a few streets from our house. His brutal attacks went on for years and it was always in the back of people's minds. For us, it came to a climax in 1979 when a 19-year-old building society clerk (Josephine Whittaker) was attacked on Savile Park Moor as she was walking home. Savile Park was a highly respectable area of town and just across the road from where I worked. The college went into high alert, with posters everywhere telling women not to walk out alone and insisting that we find walking partners at least to accompany us to the car park or a bus stop.

My evening classes finished at 9pm and normally I would have walked into town to catch a bus up to our house, but Patrick insisted that I took the bus from outside the college into

[18] So called 'Yorkshire Ripper' https://en.wikipedia.org/wiki/Peter_Sutcliffe accessed 10/05/2021

the town centre and then get a second bus that stopped at the top of our road. I tried to get the same bus each evening so that he would know what time to expect me[19]. He couldn't come to meet me because Jon was asleep in bed, but he would stand at our front door and look up the road waiting for me to walk down from the bus stop. I must admit I took to walking (sometimes running) down the middle of the road where it felt safer.

The general atmosphere of fear was compounded by the police information caravan, located in Halifax town centre at weekends, playing a recording of a man with a north-east accent who was taunting the police for not having caught him. The recording turned out to be a hoax and the attacks continued. Despite being questioned several times earlier only on minor offences, Peter Sutcliffe was finally charged in Jan 1981 with 13 cases of murder and 7 of attempted murder. There was a feeling of relief, though the whole incident had undermined mine and other women's confidence in going out alone at night - it still didn't feel that safe.

Three of us taught computing at the college; both my colleagues had worked in business before joining and they combined teaching with computer consultancy, which was an ideal arrangement. We shared a staff room with such interesting people, all so enthusiastic about their subjects – a refreshing change from my last job. I felt much more connected to the people I worked with.

The staff room was charged with energy, full of new stories, gossip and laughter. JO the geography lecturer and author of books on country walks, spent his weekends roaming the Yorkshire Dales and every Monday morning would enthuse over some new path or walkway he had discovered. TP was proud to be studying for a doctorate in English Literature, spoke

[19] There was no way of contacting him, unless I stopped at a public call box, which didn't seem that safe either.

impeccable King's English, behaved like the perfect English gentleman and would quote from Shakespeare, Hardy and Dickens in equal measures. I felt privileged when he engaged me in conversation. Then there was 'Doc,' as he insisted on being called, his doctorate in biology being wheeled out at every opportunity. Just call me 'Doc' he would say to the students in a way that made me cringe. He had an eye for the female staff, he most certainly didn't get any encouragement from me. He was in pursuit of V, the general studies teacher and feminist who lived in Hebden Bridge and was notorious for her bohemian parties. I became quite friendly with V often going out for a drink together after night school. She was great fun, made me feel rather boring but we had a good laugh. Patrick and I came into favour and were invited to one of her parties. Staffroom gossip told me that husbands may not be safe at V's house so I should keep an eye on her! She had such a magnetic personality not many people could resist her.

The maths lecturer was a beautiful French woman, not much older than me, with long black hair, a gentle manner and a radiant smile; everyone, including me, was in love with her. One day a handsome new physics lecturer arrived whose wife was supposed to be joining him in a few weeks' time, then a few weeks more, and so it went on until, at last, he had totally fallen for the maths teacher and the wife was never mentioned again. Such was the staff room, a daily delight. The head of department, Mr M, would pop into the staff room from time to time when he wanted something doing. I dreaded being called into his office, because probably it would mean more work or work I didn't want to do.

I'd been warned by the other staff to take care when I went into his office: "Never let him stand between you and the door", "Always stand near the door so that you can get out quickly" and "Never, ever go into his back room, no matter how important he makes it sound".

I took their advice and retreated in haste if he made any advances; unfortunately, that probably meant I was quicker to agree to his work-related request than I should have been.

I preferred teaching the mature students, but Mr M gave me two 'Schools Liaison' classes to teach. The idea was that a group of children, 14- or 15-years-old, would come into college one afternoon a week to learn a vocational subject, in my case computing. The two groups couldn't have been more different: one was from the boys' grammar school, wore neat blue uniforms, and were well behaved, keen to learn and competitive, wanting to finish the programming exercises quickly to impress me – such a delight; the other class was a mixed group of boys and girls from a secondary modern school, wearing whatever was in trend, mostly unwilling to learn, resenting having to come to the college and showing absolutely no interest in computing.

One afternoon, I went into the classroom to find the wastebin was on fire, several boys had their feet on the table and a portable radio was playing at the back of the room. Should I call for support? What should I do? I decided that it was either

ME or THEM. If I let them be in control, even once, then I was doomed. I left the classroom door open, put the bin outside out of sight (the fire would put itself out) and then stood squarely in the middle of the room and asked the boys to sit up; after some banter, they did. The radio was still playing; no-one would own up to whose it was, though, of course, they knew, so I just stood holding the door open, and insisted that the class would not begin until whoever had the radio left the room. I tried to appeal to the better nature of at least some of them and, eventually, the radio was at least switched off. They were 'bored', didn't understand why they were there and were just generally mischievous.

I didn't understand them, so I tried talking to some of the girls about their aspirations. One girl was ambitious to work on a sewing machine in the nearby clothes factory, because her mum and auntie worked there and she couldn't wait to join them. I learned to respect that different people had different ambitions, or maybe no ambition at all except just to live a life.

For all Mr M's faults, he did agree that I could have one day a week off for two years to attend a teacher training college to study a Certificate of Education and qualify as a higher education teacher.

At the same time, Patrick successfully completed his two-year foundation art course, passed maths and English at 'O level', achieved a grade A-star in 'A' level art and was offered a place at Leeds Polytechnic School of Art to study for a degree in graphic design.

I enjoyed my time at the college and had learnt a lot about life, about teaching and about computers, but it was again time to move on. I still had in my mind the experiences of designing systems for doctors, nurses and pathologists and wanted to explore the interface and interactions between people and computers.

Jon was ready to start school. As we were Catholics, we had decided to bring him up within the Catholic faith. There was a good infant school and church nearby and, as we had become part of the local community, it made sense to stay where we were.

Fortunately, by this time I had learned to drive, so I could now change job without moving to a new house. I had read that Huddersfield Polytechnic was seeking to expand its research profile in Computer Studies, so I duly applied for and was offered a lectureship post.

Both Patrick and I could be relatively flexible about start and end times in our new roles, so we built our schedules around dropping Jon off at school and picking him up, always making sure that one of us was there. Patrick took the train to Leeds; I drove the six miles to Huddersfield.

A new start for the three of us.

Chapter 7 It's all about cricket

I remember a conversation in the local hairdressers as I was waiting for my Mum. They were discussing who to vote for in the 1979 General Election.

One customer, sitting in front of the mirror having her hair cut, said, "Well, she is a woman; we women should stick together".

"She couldn't do much worse; at least we might have a full week of electricity", the hairdresser replied, referring to the miners' strikes and three-day week[20] of the Callaghan[21] era.

Another customer under the hairdryer added, "It's about time we had a woman as Prime Minister. Imagine that: a woman as Prime Minister. I don't normally vote Tory, but I think I'll vote for her."

Margaret Thatcher won the election and became the first female Prime Minister (PM); it had taken nearly 260[22] years and 49 male PMs for a woman to take the highest office in the UK. It seemed to herald a change for women.

I don't know whether the woman under the hairdryer was happy with her decision, but as the 1980s unfolded, we were to see great change: deregulation of financial markets, privatisation of state-owned companies, reduction in the power of trade unions and weakening of the UK computer industry.

It was a time of great change for me too.

---

[20] Due to widespread trade union strikes in late 1970s there was only enough electricity for businesses to operate for three days a week. They had to close on the other two days.

[21] James Callaghan, UK Prime Minister 1976-1979, leader of the Labour Party 1976-1980.

[22] Sir Robert Walpole was the first British Prime Minister appointed in 1721.

I joined the Department of Computer Studies and Mathematics [23] at Huddersfield Polytechnic as a Lecturer, with a view to launching my research career. My passion was to understand more about the interaction between people and computers and to investigate how I might impact the design of future systems.

My initial teaching schedule consisted mainly of teaching programming and running practical labs. I taught Microsoft BASIC[24] and COBOL 74[25] and, though I had no previous experience of either, found that having learned several computer languages in the past it was relatively easy to learn another.

The students were keen and class sizes were only around 60, so great for getting to know the students individually.

The staff were friendly with a mix of mathematicians, operations researchers and systems analysts. The systems analysts were the most fun; a group of three shared an office and I'd often pop in at lunchtime. Invariably they were playing table tennis across the desks or football with the door as goalposts. They would read from Private Eye and make me laugh. I enjoyed their departmental political banter and learnt a lot about how things really worked: how to lobby to change the syllabus to reflect your own research interests; how to get funding to go to research meetings; how to get past the deputy head to get what you wanted from the head of department.

---

[23] The Polytechnic in Huddersfield, West Yorkshire specialised in STEM subjects (science, technology, engineering and maths). Later to become The University of Huddersfield

[24] Microsoft BASIC: Beginner's All-Purpose Symbolic Instruction Code: a programming language popular for home computers in the late 1970s early 1980s.

[25] COBOL 74: Common Business Oriented Language: uses English like statements, designed for business use.

In the early 1980s, my research area was broadly known as 'Man Machine Interface' and originated in the design of controls for machines, such as the cockpit of an aeroplane, but later to become known as 'Human Computer Interaction' or HCI.

There was some interest in HCI in the department and the head was supportive in my developing the area. I looked to the British Computer Society and attended their Special Interest Group (SIG) in HCI. Unfortunately, all their meetings were held in London, mostly in the evenings and not convenient to attend. I reached out to people in the North of England and formed a Northern HCI SIG. We organised monthly meetings with speakers active in HCI research, later including Expert Systems[26].

We were fortunate that the Joint Academic Network (JANET) gave email access to universities in the early eighties, and we were able to arrange meetings. In 1980 mobile phones were as big as bricks and digital mobile phones were not yet available[27].

Organising the meetings was extra work for me, but an invaluable way of finding out about research in HCI and having the opportunity to speak about my own interests. It was through this networking that I found out about the UK Alvey Programme.

The Alvey Programme was a research programme sponsored by the government in response to the Japanese Fifth

---

[26] An expert system is a computer system that emulates the decision-making ability of a human expert, mainly reasoning through use of if-then statements

[27] In fact, by 1982 only about 50% of households had a telephone of any kind

Generation[28] project; it ran from 1983 to 1990 and its primary aim was the improvement of advanced information technology in the UK. The Department of Trade and Industry (DTI) and the Science and Engineering Research Council (SERC) jointly administered Alvey with funding for five areas of research,[29] of which 'Man-Machine Interface' was one.

I attended meetings in London designed to inform the research community of Alvey's goals and stimulate response from universities and industry. The programme as a whole looked very technical and I wasn't sure if my ideas would fit, but I was greatly encouraged by discussions with Professor Ernest Edmonds[30]. His enthusiasm for HCI was infectious, and I was in awe that he had already published research on 'Adaptive Man-Computer Interfaces' [10]. He was an artist at heart with a unique talent in art, creativity, and human-computer interaction: a beautiful, generous man.

With Professor Edmonds' endorsement ringing in my ears, I travelled back north and set to work on my first research proposal: title, aims, previous research, method, expected outcomes, beneficiaries, resources, plan, milestones, deliverables - quite a task! My first competitive bid for research funds.

---

[28] The term "fifth generation" was intended to convey the system as being a leap beyond existing machines. The definition of 'generation' varies, but in terms of hardware generation one used vacuum tubes, two used transistors and diodes, three used integrated circuits and the fourth generation used microprocessors.

[29] Focus areas for the Alvey Programme included: VLSI (very large scale integration) technology for microelectronics, Artificial Intelligence, Software Engineering, Man-Machine Interface and Systems Architecture

[30] http://www.ernestedmonds.com accessed 10/05/2021

The title was 'Adaptive Dialogues at the Man-Machine Interface', and the aim was to investigate how to design a single user interface that adapts to the needs of different types of users. Not being a Psychologist, I realised I would need help in understanding how to define 'different types of users'. Dr Chris Fowler, from the Department of Behavioural Science at Huddersfield and an expert in Cognitive Psychology, came to the rescue and became a key source of inspiration and subsequent co-investigator.

After a great deal of work, the competitive funding bid was successful and gave Chris and me enough resources to employ one programmer and one research assistant for three years and to buy two ICL PERQ computers running UNIX.

I shared an office with one of the two other female academic staff members; her specialisation was Operations Research working mainly on transport scheduling and optimisation. My 'Adaptive Dialogues' project would need daily interaction between Chris, myself and the team, and space for equipment and experiments. Sharing an office just wasn't practical.

The deputy head of department, Mr Taylor was in charge of departmental resources, including room allocation. *(He preferred to be addressed as 'Mr')* Of course, he already knew about the success of the Alvey award, a source of great kudos for the department.

I explained why we needed space, how much space and that I wanted to set up an HCI Research Lab to grow the research area.

His response was, "It's not all about Geoff Boycott[31] you know, Linda".

I looked at him bemused, not being sure who Geoff Boycott was, though vaguely aware he might be a cricketer.

---

[31] Geoff Boycott played Test cricket for Yorkshire and England from 1962 to 1986

"It's the team," he said. "You have to play for the team. You might be a high scorer, but don't think you can have it all your own way."
What was he trying to say? How should I respond? I am not Geoff Boycott! Perhaps he'd been listening to England test cricket on the radio before I entered his office. I really should have paid more attention to cricket. I'd been to a match, once, and found it so slow that I lost interest. Clearly, other people, especially the Deputy Head, found it very exciting and it absorbed their every thought.

I could see that to have a meaningful conversation with Mr Taylor I would need to speak to him in cricket metaphors. I was clearly on a 'sticky wicket' asking him for resources directly.

That first meeting made me feel that I was doing something unjust to my colleagues, simply 'not cricket', and that I would need to go back with a different approach.

I was only asking for a room! Albeit a large one.

What was my strategy to be?

First, I would go to the head of department and explain that it was a condition of my award that the Polytechnic provided suitable space and ask him to have a word with Mr Taylor. If that didn't work then the three systems analysts suggested that I should bribe him. Not directly with cash of course but by giving him something he wanted. If I could help him bring money into the department then maybe his success would soften his attitude towards me. I could introduce him to one of my industry collaborators who had expressed potential interest in financial support. Maybe that would work? This may seem like a lot of effort, but the alternative was to brush up on cricket and I knew that had me 'stumped'.

I duly arranged a meeting between myself, Mr Taylor, and my industry contact, Peter Ward. After some banter about cricket (I had no idea what they were talking about) Mr Ward said, "We recently introduced computer systems throughout our organisation, and now have a wide range of non-technical users, a number of whom are, quite frankly, finding things difficult".

Mr Taylor: "Yes I can appreciate that."

Peter: "We are interested in the work Linda and her colleagues are doing in user interface design and would like to collaborate with a view to improving the user experience in our future systems."

So far so good.

Mr T: "What did you have in mind?"

Peter: "Collaboration; involvement with the research team. If we could offer some financial contribution, what would be your ideal?"

Oh really, I hadn't expected this! I hadn't primed Mr T for this!

Mr T: "Well, it would be wonderful if you could donate a student prize, maybe £50?"

Oh no! £50! How embarrassing! I was in the wrong place.

Peter looked at me somewhat confused; he was expecting to be asked for £5000, £10,000 or £20,000 research sponsorship but not £50 for undergrads! He decided he was in the wrong place too, and started backing towards the door. Conversation over, maybe in his own little way Mr Taylor was impressed but

Peter Ward wasn't. He was interested in our research but not in the department. An important lesson for me was to prepare for a meeting better and to be ready to manage the conversation.

Mr Taylor did get his £50 for the student prize and was exceedingly pleased with himself. He eventually assigned a laboratory and a small suite of rooms to our HCI Research Unit, so maybe all was not lost.

The aim of the Adaptive Dialogues project was to investigate the relationship between individual differences and user interface design.

The doctors, nurses and pharmacists were still in my mind from earlier experiences. All computer users are not the same; yet the people who design computers for them tend to be very similar, in that they are computer experts or programmers and mostly male. People typically design for people who are like themselves, and I wanted to find out if designing differently for different types of user made any difference.

I was most excited about the new computers purchased for the project. The ICL PERQ 1 was a stand-alone workstation running the UNIX operating system with a Graphical User Interface that would give us flexibility to experiment with different user interface designs. We programmed using the language PASCAL.

As a Behavioural Scientist Chris advised us on how to formulate hypotheses, recruit subjects, and design and conduct experiments. He pointed us towards Cognitive Style as a way of measuring psychological differences between individuals. It is a concept used in Cognitive Psychology to describe the way individuals think, perceive and remember information.

There are a number of dimensions within Cognitive Style but because we were investigating different ways of presenting information we decided to focus on field-dependence and field-independence. Typically, a field-dependent person tends to have difficulty finding a shape hidden in a background of lines of other shapes, but they are also more likely to have good interpersonal skills, read social cues and openly convey their feelings. Field-dependent people notice a lack of structure in the environment and are more affected by it than other people. [11]

By contrast, a field-independent person can easily impose their own sense of order in a situation lacking structure. They are also observed to function autonomously in social situations and are sometimes described as impersonal and task-oriented.

We recruited 40 administrative staff from across the Polytechnic to take part in the experiments.

Most people were unfamiliar with using computers, the administrative staff mostly using electronic typewriters and manual filing systems. Personal computers were very much in the ascendency in the early 1980s but more likely to be used by the home hobbyist, e.g. Sinclair ZX80, or college students, e.g. Acorn BBC Micro or Commodore 64, than by mainstream administrators. It was the IBM Personal Computer that led the way onto the office desk following its launch in 1981 but hadn't yet reached the Polytechnic.

We used two examples of user interface design, command line and menu-driven. Command line interfaces are text-based, and users control the computer by typing in commands one line at a time; the user has to remember the name of the command and the syntax of the instruction and to decide how instructions flow one from another. Menu-driven interfaces present users with a list of choices from a menu; there is no need to remember syntax and the computer controls how the user navigates through the options available, thus providing a ready-made structure.

To assess whether staff were field-dependent or field-independent Chris administered the GEFT test. GEFT [12] stands for the Group Embedded Figures Test and is a timed psychological assessment to assess the position of an individual on the spectrum.

Our hypothesis was that field-independent people would perform better and prefer the command line interface, and that field-dependent people would perform better and prefer the menu-driven interface.

If the hypothesis proved to be true, we would then design a User Interface Management System that would allow the interface design to adapt according to the preferences and psychological profile of the user.

All this preparation took place in 1982 with the project proper to start in earnest in January 1983.

Towards the end of 1982 I found I was expecting a second child. Fortunately, I kept well, had a glowing feeling most of the time and was able to get the project up and running. My clothes got bigger, and I became slower at moving around, so I was glad to leave for the statutory ten weeks before the baby was due. I was overwhelmed by the leaving party, with so many people, gifts and good wishes. I didn't think I was 'leaving' but it seemed that everyone else did.

It was eight years since I last gave birth and thought I might have forgotten what to do! I conscientiously attended the antenatal classes and learned about breathing and staying in control. It all worked wonderfully, still painful of course, but I genuinely felt in control of my body and able to do as the midwife asked. Patrick was there the whole time and delighted to be the first to see our beautiful baby girl: a wondrous sister for Jon.

Theresa was born in May 1983, perfect in every way. 'Deo Gratias'[32] were the words iced onto a pure white Christening cake made by our next-door neighbour. They had seven children and probably thought we would never have another one.

[32] 'Deo Gratias' is Latin for 'Thanks be to God'

Maternity leave officially finished six weeks after the birth; I was due back in July when the students were on holiday. Excellent timing! I could take until mid-September to return full-time, just going in to make sure all was well with the HCI Research Unit.

Patrick was as positive as ever about looking after the baby. He continued to pursue his artwork whenever he got time, but realistically there wasn't going to be much of that for a while.

September arrived and I returned to work expecting my regular teaching workload, only to find that I had been given an extra class: a 12-hour, 6-week course to teach computer programming to a class of politics students. It crossed my mind that Mr Taylor might have it in for me, but I didn't complain and thought there may be something for me to learn. After all, anyone can learn to write computer code, or could they?

The decision had been taken to teach them the programming language COBOL: not a bad decision as it had English-like statements and was designed to be readable by businesspeople. The students hadn't been assigned any practical lab time, so they wrote their programs on coding sheets and submitted them for processing.

The COBOL program below asks the user to enter two numbers, multiplies them together and displays the result.

```
PROCEDURE DIVISION.
    DISPLAY "Enter first number  (1 digit) : " WITH NO
ADVANCING.
    ACCEPT Num1.
    DISPLAY "Enter second number (1 digit) : " WITH NO
ADVANCING.
    ACCEPT Num2.
    MULTIPLY Num1 BY Num2 GIVING Result.
    DISPLAY "Result is = ", Result.
    STOP RUN.
```

The English words used as instructions are clear enough; DISPLAY means display on the screen, ACCEPT means accept the input from the user, and so on. The politics students could grasp these easily enough, but they struggled with the idea of syntax. Syntax requires attention to detail: the language specifies that each line must end in a full stop, instructions must be in CAPITAL LETTERS, and there must be a space between each part of the instruction. They would submit their program and invariably it would come back with errors 'period missing in line 7', 'syntax error line 10', and they were so frustrated.

Try as I might, there was a group of students who just couldn't cope. "Why do I need to include a full-stop or a space; why can't the computer work it out for itself?", or "I thought computers were supposed to be smart".

Well, they are only as smart as their programmers! There isn't much debate about the syntax of a programming language; the person who wrote the Compiler[33] sets the rules and your program won't compile if you don't follow them.

The politics students really struggled with rules and syntax, and it seemed to me that they would never learn to program unless we designed an entirely new kind of programming language: a programming language that our future politicians could learn. Technology was changing so fast that it seemed to me that everyone should learn to program.

I was still driving ahead with the research too. With two exceptions, my academic colleagues were men; most seemed surprised to see me back after the summer holiday but there I was.

---

[33] A Compiler is a program that converts instructions into a machine-code or lower-level form so that they can be read and executed by a computer. Grace Hopper wrote the first COBOL compiler in the 1960s.

One aspect of the 'Adaptive Dialogues' project that I found particularly fascinating was the way we were able to monitor keystrokes: not only which keys had been pressed but also at what time. In practice this meant that we could write software to report upon precisely what the user was doing while they carried out the experimental tasks. We could see which keys they pressed; if they were typing in a command we could see if they made a mistake, what kind of mistake it was, how many times they tried to correct it and how long it took them to arrive at the correct command. We could also analyse gaps between keyboard entries, measure 'thinking time' and try to interpret what they were doing between gaps in keyboard depressions. I found this ability to monitor the user's every action and every thought both exciting and worrying, as I hadn't encountered anything similar before. Nevertheless, it gave us lots of data that told us how well a given user was performing with a given user interface design.

In addition to the keystroke data, we collected more subjective data in the form of user satisfaction questionnaires, i.e. how the users felt about their experience with a given design.

One difficulty with the project was recruiting people to take part, because the whole process for one person took about three hours and we had to negotiate with various heads of school to give their staff time off. Almost all of 1983 was taken up conducting experiments and analysing the results.

The final results showed a high correlation between the level of satisfaction and performance of field-dependent people when using the menu-driven interface, while field-independent people generally preferred and performed better with the command line. Our hypothesis was proved to be correct and the evidence re-affirmed the need for the user interface to adapt to individual differences.

Towards the end of 1983, I was expecting our third child. I tried not to look so big this time and, given that I was still trying to shed the weight from Theresa's birth, no-one really noticed.

I saw the academic year 1983/84 through from September to June then took maternity leave for a second time. Colleagues didn't have much appetite for a 'leaving do' this time, no doubt worrying that this was to be an annual occurrence.

I didn't feel quite so glowing and was pleased to have some time at home with Jon, Theresa and Patrick. My attendance at antenatal classes was intermittent; I felt confident I would remember what to do, for after all it was only a year ago.

However, when I got into the delivery room, I couldn't remember a single thing: how to breathe, when to breathe, what to do when the midwife told me to push. I just couldn't control my body. The midwife started to get worried and looked at Patrick. He was standing next to me, and I have no idea what he said, but whatever he said, I did. Patrick was totally in control of my body; I breathed when he said, I pushed when he said, I stopped when he said and eventually the baby came. The midwife was astonished, saying she had never seen two people so connected.

She was a very special baby with red hair, blue eyes, pale skin and freckles: a true redhead. We both have dark brown hair, so naturally people joked, saying, "Is she the milkman's daughter?[34]". Oddly enough, our milkman did have ginger hair, but the truth is that my older sister and brother have red hair and it runs through my side of the family.

Our wonderful daughter, who we named Christine, was born in July, allowing me to stretch my maternity leave from six weeks to ten weeks before returning for the new academic year 1984/85.

---

[34] An old joke used when a child doesn't look like the rest of the family. A milkman delivered milk daily to the doorstep of a house (and sometimes went in!!)

Chapter 8 The whole thing was absurd

Bob Geldof and 'Live Aid' lit up the summer of 1985 in a wave of excitement and generosity, raising over £30 million for famine relief in Africa. Legends[35] gave free performances; the public gave money[36].
Live television was broadcast to 1.5 billion viewers worldwide for the first time. Technology was advancing rapidly, with automated cash machines outside the banks, scanners at the supermarket checkout and tabletop games to entertain the children.

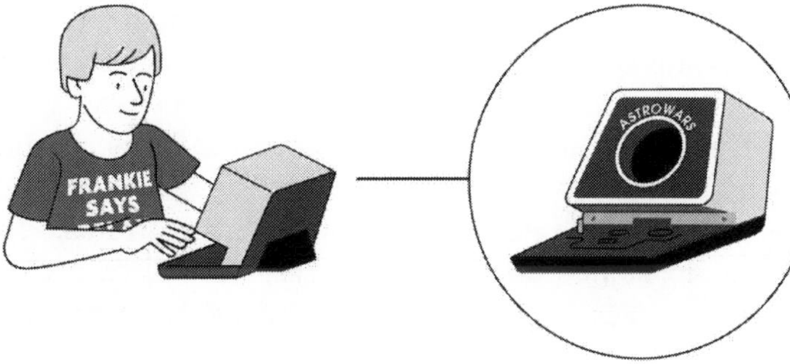

Astrowars: electronic tabletop game by Grandstand -1980s

Computer terminals, connected via data links, heralded a shift away from centralised computing towards greater decentralisation and an increase in non-specialist computer users. Clerical workers were expected to increase efficiency and

[35] Including David Bowie, Queen, U2, The Who, Rolling Stones, Black Sabbath …

[36] Those lucky enough to attend the live show paid £25 a ticket, despite many jobs paying £1.20 an hour or less.

do more work for the same amount of pay. Their every keystroke was monitored and analysed.

While the majority of clerical workers were female very few women were involved in the design or programming of these new systems. 'By the late 1980s working with computers had acquired a distinctly masculine image in British society' [13] and, unsurprisingly, the number of female computer science graduates and programmers was in steady decline.

The Polytechnic at Huddersfield fared slightly better with around 30% of the students on the 'Computing in Business' degree programme being female.

Much of my department's work was of an applied nature, which I liked very much. I particularly enjoyed project work and getting teams of students to work on an industry problem over a prolonged period.

The Polytechnic had a system of points for measuring staff workload and to ensure a fair distribution of work between members of the same department; research grants, doctoral students, masters students and undergrads all earned points. This meant that the more research I did the less teaching I had to do. Mr Taylor, who we met in chapter 7, wasn't too keen on my having such a 'privileged' timetable and, of course, this was a source of some contention for me. Realistically you can't do both well. I was determined to continue my HCI research, and persuaded him to agree to my sharing the teaching load with my research assistants, where in any case it was good for their own development to tutor undergrads a few hours each week. I put my teaching energy into developing a new taught course on HCI.

I'd thought about leaving around this time; I'd just had two babies and was still in recovery mode. I remember saying to a friend that it was not so much that I was getting older but that I was becoming more and more tired. Patrick was amazing but, really, I did need to get home in the evening and do my bit around the house at the weekends. My son Jon was nine years old and had football, karate and other interests that needed parental attention. Patrick was quite sporty himself, having been captain of both football and athletics teams at school. He became a coach for the local junior football team and was notorious for running up and down the touchline shouting at the top of his voice, "Move into position", "Pull back", "Use your area" at the same time rebuking unruly parents as they shouted, "Take him out" or "Break his leg", provoking those on the opposite side of the pitch.

However, I felt there was some momentum building in the research and I continued to network and build up contacts, getting more traction from industry practitioners. The British Library was interested in our work. They were looking at the possibility of offering computer terminals[37] within the library to enable members of the public to search the library catalogue. They were concerned that the library staff's expert method of searching wouldn't be appropriate and wanted to experiment with different types of interface, depending on the profile of the user. Profiles identified were students, teachers and researchers. These were arrived at using a set of questions, with interfaces adapted appropriately: an early example of collecting profiles and user experience data to adapt what the user sees on the screen. This was the beginning of Online Public Access to library Catalogues (OPAC) and our project was called 'Matching OPAC User Interfaces to User Needs'.

Evaluation was an important aspect of our research; how did users feel? How did they react when trying to use the newly designed system? It was clear that it was difficult to predict how a user would react, whether they would use all the features you'd designed, whether it would fit with their everyday work or even whether they would use it as you intended. You were

[37] The computer terminals were connected directly to the library's mainframe computer (the internet not yet available)

always designing for a future situation; no-one knew precisely what that would be. You may be designing something now that wouldn't be completed or given to the user for a year or more. You needed to be able to predict the future.

Large companies had particular difficulties, often developing generic products that could be used by more than one customer. How could you design a system to meet the needs of users across a range of organisations? We had discussed these problems with Dr Andrew Hutt from the HCI Group at International Computers Limited (ICL) and decided that we should collaborate to develop a user-centred method that ICL product designers could apply to help them foresee the needs of users.

We worked on a funding bid to SERC[38] to obtain the resources to do the research. It was to be a method that could be applied in practice and developed using real-life product teams. The proposal was successful and represented another major award for my HCI Research Unit.

The Unit was growing, attracting doctoral students, and increasingly being seen as a flagship research centre for the department. I was promoted to Principal Lecturer and it seemed all the hard work was bearing fruit, but I was ready for a rest. In fact, by the May bank holiday of 1985, the whole family felt ready for a break, and the five of us set off to the Flower of May holiday park near Scarborough. It was ideally placed in open country, yet close to the seaside, had entertainment for Jon (swimming, tenpin bowling, a games room) and a play area for Theresa and Christine.

One evening, Patrick took Jon to the sports bar to watch the European Cup Final between his beloved Liverpool and the Italian football team Juventus, played at the Heysel Stadium in Brussels, on 29th May 1985. They were only gone about half an

[38] The UK Science and Engineering Research Council https://epsrc.ukri.org/about/history/ourbeginnings/ accessed 10/05/2021

hour when they returned looking distraught. There had been a terrible disaster with fans being crushed against a wall and dying. Patrick brought Jon away as soon as he saw what was unfolding as only two weeks earlier 56 football fans had died in the Bradford Stadium fire and we were all still in a state of shock. Bradford is only seven miles from Halifax, and we knew people who had been there.

We decided that watching television, even the football, wasn't such a good idea while we were on holiday. The countryside, sea, sand and children's entertainment were enough, and we enjoyed the rest of the holiday.

Back at work, it was time to start our new project called 'User Skills and Task Match', not a great title but it did represent what we were trying to do, i.e. match the design of a computer product to the skills of users and the tasks they had to carry out within an organisation. Andrew's vision was to address the earliest stages of the design process where the specification of the new product was being decided, in other words to 'design the right product', namely one that users and organisations would benefit from.

To this end, senior staff with decision-making authority such as designers, programmers, technical authors and marketing staff were brought together in a workshop-style meeting. Andrew wanted Chris[39] and me to act as professional facilitators, guiding the workshop members through our structured user-centred design method. As professional facilitators we were there to assist the group achieve its aims, while having no stake in the outcome.

We would get together, staying in a hotel for three days, usually in Reading or London. The first day would be spent 'exploring the user environment' - in other words getting them to understand the target user of the proposed product, their

[39] Dr Chris Fowler, Behavioural Scientist, mentioned in chapter 7

knowledge and skills, their current job and how it would change, and benefits for the organisation. At the end of the first day a 'typical' user was invited to dinner and asked further questions to validate or otherwise the outcome of the first day.

At one workshop, the group had identified the computer operator as their target user. The illustration shows computer operators and computer room typical of the time.

Typical computer room for the ICL2900 series showing exchangeable disk packs – dates from 1984

The overall goal of the group was to raise the level of automation of the operating system itself, and hence reduce the number of interventions needed by the operator - known as an 'ease-of-use front end'.

A typical computer operator was invited to dinner. The group had been briefed not to mention the proposed product, but simply to ask the user about his everyday job.

Marketeer: "Thank you for coming. We have a few questions for you. First, could you tell us about yourself, your job title, skills and background?"

User: "I'm a senior computer operator and have worked with the ICL 2966 series for a number of years."

Designer: "What do you do on a typical day?"

User: "I follow on-screen messages issued by the operating system, adjust settings, control workflow and issue instructions to junior operators to change disk packs and load paper into the printer. We also watch and listen to the computer for signs of problems. We intervene to prevent downtime."

Designer: "Can you say a little more about your day; is there a sequence of tasks?"

User: "Haha! I think I know what you are working on! I've seen the promotional video!"

At this point everyone looked astonished. He'd seen the promotional video. How could that be, they hadn't even decided what the proposed product was going to do yet?

A quick look at the group by Andrew said 'say nothing' to the user.

The group made light of the situation over dinner but were worried and confused as none of them had seen the video.

The sales team had made a promotional video based purely on the concept of a new version of the operating system. No design decisions had actually been made, no set of requirements documented. The workshop group were under tremendous pressure.

On the second day we examined the tasks users carried out at that time, how they would change with the proposed new product and what benefits or otherwise might accrue. In addition, we examined objects the user handled throughout the day[40] and how they would change. By the end of the day, the

[40] Examples of 'objects': if discussing a payroll system an object might be a ledger or a payslip. If discussing an airline system an object might be a ticket,

group had examined the user and discussed the proposed product from three points of view - the user, tasks and objects - and were beginning to understand what their product must do to achieve benefits for both user and organisation. They spent the evening preparing a presentation for their Product Manager on user requirements, describing what the product should do and the design outline which they presented on day three.

Various outcomes could ensue: they could agree on the way forward, make amendments or on occasion cancel the project altogether if they could see no benefit.

In the case of the 'ease-of-use front end', the Project Manager arrived literally with a cheque in his top pocket ready to commission a software house to build the product. The workshop had been very successful, despite the fact that the ideal of a full product description was not achieved. The team had made sufficient progress, agreed on an initial design and had an understanding of how they would proceed with the rest of it.

It was interesting to learn where product ideas came from. It could be a new version of an existing product, a product to rival that of a competitor or some new technology that the company had developed and which they needed to find a use for.

Users were an important link between marketing and design, and the user-centred method provided an efficient and structured means of investigation. ICL eventually adopted the method as their own and called it 'Marketing to Design'.

Learning to be a facilitator was great fun, though extremely demanding. Andrew had great faith in us and our user-centred method and paid us each £1,000 a day for our efforts. I imagine this was a fairly standard professional

---

a boarding pass or a passenger list. In the case of an operating system objects include discs, printers, job lists – anything the computer operator would handle or interact with

consultancy fee for the mid-to-late eighties, but it was a great boost to my self-confidence.

Chris and I would work together throughout the day; he would focus on the user level and myself on the tasks and object level. Chris could answer questions related to the underlying psychology whilst I had a better grasp of technical computer issues discussed.

As a professional facilitator, I would guide the group discussion through the stages of the method, at the same time monitoring the discussion, recognising when problems were developing, being ready to intervene and use all my knowledge and skills to deal with the problem, so that the group could continue to make progress. I read a great deal about professional facilitation [14] and learned to recognise the generic problem syndromes described by professional facilitators such as the 'multi-headed beast', 'feuding factions', 'dominant species', 'recycling' and the 'sleeping meeting' syndromes.

Fortunately, we rarely encountered the 'multi-headed beast' syndrome, where participants would try to hijack the agenda to their own ends causing digressions or multiple topics. Our user-centred design method was the agenda and we reinforced that throughout the day.

The most common problem was the 'feuding factions' syndrome, typically caused by hidden agendas, power struggles or fear of change. This was hardly surprising since the jobs of the product teams at the workshop could be affected by the outcome, for example, if the product were cancelled or changed direction. Often, two or three members would stand in a corner over coffee and agree their preferred outcome and then try to impose it on the rest of the group which could lead to open attacks, anger or repetitious arguments while they tried to get their own way. One way of dealing with this was to stop the discussion and get each individual to list their criteria for success; namely in this case the criteria should relate to the users and not to their own self-interest. We had to keep re-affirming that the success of the product depended on its benefits for the users!

The next most common was the 'dominant species' syndrome, where one or two people dominated the discussion and others became frustrated or withdrawn because they were not heard. One intervention would be to do a 'round robin' to get each person to say something and limit their time for contribution.

Occasionally the 'recycling' syndrome would arise within one of the sessions if there was irritation with lack of progress or failure to gain consensus. Ideas might not be being sufficiently recorded and there was a need to re-affirm where we were, where we'd been and where we were up to.

The 'sleeping meeting' syndrome sometimes occurred after lunch! This could mean long silences, absence of energy or ideas or withdrawal. It could just be fatigue, or, more worrying, hostility or fear of a volatile issue.

On the whole, the workshop participants were cooperative, after all it was important to them that they should be part of the decision-making process. Only once, a participant got really angry, slammed his fist on the table, knocked over a chair and stormed out of the room. I didn't know what to do, for I hadn't encountered so much anger in my life. My first instinct was to let him go, then try to calm the room. Chris agreed; we did a quick summary of where we were up to and carried on with the session. Fortunately, Andrew was there himself and understood how to deal with it, reassured the rest of the group, and said the person would not be returning to the workshop. Andrew told us later that the man had 'issues' to be resolved with his superiors.

I found the workshops fascinating because there was so much going on and so many things to think about all at once. Not only had you to guide the group through the process but you also had to listen to each of them, assimilate what they were saying, see if the discussion was developing in the right way and if not, why not, and if intervention were needed. You also had to be aware of your own performance; everyone was looking at you, how you were dressed, how you spoke, how you reacted to what they said. You had to be aware of the politics going on in the room; occasionally we had a briefing with a senior person, before the workshop, giving us some background to the project and the people attending and forewarning us of possible problems. There were physical and technical things to deal with such as projectors, white boards and flip charts; everything had to work well. Socially we had breakfast, lunch, coffee and evening meals with the group, so it was important to hold conversations and be sensitive to what was said and, of course, use your knife and fork properly and have a sense of humour at all times.

I was invariably the only woman in the room throughout the day, but it didn't seem to matter as I was there in a professional capacity, endorsed by senior management, and confident in my knowledge and skills. It would have been nice to have other women there if only for the occasional woman-to-woman chat.

I enjoyed the paid consultancy, bought some new dining room furniture and treated myself to an Apple Mac Plus and printer.

Apple Mac Plus with external floppy disc drive and mouse – 1987

Unfortunately, the Polytechnic didn't like my doing paid consultancy and took 60% of my earnings, leaving me only 40% from which I had to pay tax. I argued that the consultancy was related to research and would enhance prospects of future collaborations with ICL, but, no, they didn't think I should use Polytechnic time in this way. Chris and I were not happy; it was barely worth all the hard work for just over £200 a day. We decided to set up our own consultancy business and register with ICL as a preferred supplier; we called it 'People and Computers'. This way we had only the taxman to pay out and it made it easier to do work for other clients.

The HCI Research Unit was continuing to build in strength, with doctoral students adding to our number. I had ideas about the next phase of the research, wanting to look at ways of running our user-centred design workshops remotely, using technology to enable the teams to work together to make decisions or have arguments and discussions without physically meeting. Also, and more exciting for me, was to develop computer support for the role of the facilitator. Full of ideas about the next research project, I began to look for funding sources.

At that time everyone was talking about ESPRIT[41], a European research programme with major funding for information technology. The overall idea of the ESPRIT programme was to bring together researchers to share their knowledge and expertise to achieve European strategic goals in information technology, research and development. Having read the programme and goals, I could see a heading under 'Human Computer Interaction' that matched my ideas. Unlike the UK SERC programme, where I could just collaborate within the UK, ESPRIT meant that I had to have European partners. I knew of European researchers in HCI but had never met them personally. Fortunately, there was to be an information event where you could go to Brussels, hear about the part of the programme that interested you, meet up with others with similar interests, hopefully hit it off and collaborate in producing a joint funding bid.

I spoke to the head of department to request funds to travel to Brussels for three days to meet and develop relationships with fellow (yet unknown) European HCI researchers. Yes, he said, that's good. Then he said, 'But I can only afford for one person to go from the department, so can you represent the work of other staff while you are there?' I was somewhat befuddled by this request; how could I represent the Information Systems group or the Operations Research group? But this is what he wanted and was a condition of my going.

---

[41] European Strategic Programme on Research in Information Technology (ESPRIT) was a series of integrated programmes of information technology research and development projects and industrial technology transfer measures. Five ESPRIT programmes (ESPRIT 0 to ESPRIT 4) ran consecutively from 1983 to 1998.

As if that wasn't enough, I was called to see the Head of Research for the whole Polytechnic. 'You have asked for funding to go to the ESPRIT information event? Such a good idea but really, to justify you going, I need you to represent other departments, especially Textiles and Engineering.'

I arrived in Brussels with a presentation about my own research, in case I got chance to speak in front of the HCI group, and loaded with documents of varying sizes representing what seemed like the whole of the Polytechnic.

There were thousands of people at the event. HCI was divided across a number of rooms; which should I attend? I needed three of me just to find out what was going on in HCI! Other people were more savvy than me; clearly, some partnerships had already been formed and they were using the opportunity to meet and take their proposal to the next level. I was way behind!

I had a chance lift conversation with three academics from Manchester:

"So, you are here on your own?" they smirked.

"Yes."

"…and you are from 'uddersfield?" They cracked up with laughter.

"Yes, I am."

"You are very brave; have you worked out which session to attend?'

"No, I have to represent Textiles and Engineering as well as Information Systems, and my own area of HCI."

More laughter!

At this point I was laughing too; the whole thing was absurd.

They each represented solely their own interests and that was hard enough.

'You should join us; why not move to UMIST[42]?' was their departing shot.

The trip to Brussels totally re-affirmed my feeling that the Polytechnic was the wrong place for me. I had benefitted a great deal from having the freedom to pursue my research passion and had developed personally and professionally. I felt there was no more room for growth, and it was time to move on.

I talked to Mum to see if she could help out but at the time she still lived in Burnley. In the early 1970s the town council had compulsory purchased the small terraced house, where I was raised, to make way for a new motorway. She was given the princely sum of £900, not enough to buy another house, so was forced to move into a council flat. Never having had so much money, she spent a few happy years enjoying holidays abroad and buying that new furniture she always wanted but could never afford. We would drive across to see her at weekends, a lovely drive through the hills and winding roads via Hebden Bridge and Todmorden. (Lovely, that is, if your son isn't being sick every 5 minutes.) The journey often took much longer than the allotted 50 minutes, but we loved being at Grandma's; she was so warm and loving, making us all feel special.

Towards the end of the 1980s, with the girls approaching school age, Mum decided she would move over to Halifax to help us out. At first she stayed with us but with intervention from my sister, Sheila, Halifax housing department offered her a flat of her own. Her new flat was just near the school bus stop, and she could see the girls onto the bus in the morning and be there to meet them after school. We paid her of course. Everyone was happy to have Mum nearby and more involved in our lives. She had her own life too, and soon established a circle of friends through church, bridge club and charitable activities.

[42] UMIST: the University of Manchester Institute of Science and Technology

Patrick now felt he could return to paid work. At first, we thought it would be difficult for Patrick to find work after so many years at home looking after the children, but it didn't take long before the offers rolled in. We laughed at one offer, selling double-glazing by knocking on house doors. Patrick looked the absolute opposite of the clean-shaven, collar-and-tie rep you'd expect. What a shock if they saw him with his long hair and beard! As it turned out, they didn't want him for door-to-door sales, but to manage a fleet of such salesmen - a bit nearer the mark. In the end he accepted a job as a yard foreman in a building firm to manage the building stock. The bosses had spotted something special in him - an honest man! Builders were notorious for helping themselves to stock to do jobs on the side. It needed all his charm and tact to become as popular as he did with both bosses and builders.

Not only did Mum being there before and after school mean that Patrick could work it also meant I was able to look further afield for a better job.

Chapter 9 What's in it for me?

It was 1989 and, for as long as I could remember, the Cold War was part of the backdrop to my life, with continual rumblings of tension between the United States and Soviet Russia. It was a great relief when in late Autumn 1989 the symbol of division between East and West, the Berlin Wall, began to be dismantled brick by brick. Margaret Thatcher, together with US President George Bush Senior and Soviet leader Mikhail Gorbachev declared the end of the Cold War.

I can still hear Roger Waters[43] of Pink Floyd performing 'The Wall - Live in Berlin' in a rock concert celebrating the fall of the wall - daringly staged in the former 'no-man's-land' where people had risked their lives to escape from East to West Germany.

The same year saw the introduction of the Poll Tax, which contributed to Margaret Thatcher's own downfall after ten years in office. The Poll Tax was an attempt to replace the system of 'rates' - a tax on property that had been in place for centuries - with taxation on the individual. There were mass protests across Britain because it disproportionally taxed the poor in favour of the rich. So strong were the feelings in our neighbourhood that

[43] https://en.wikipedia.org/wiki/Roger_Waters

our local priest staged a sit-in in protest and was arrested for his part in the 'Poll Tax riots'[44].

This momentous year also saw the birth of the internet and the dawn of a new era in technology. The English computer scientist, Tim Berners-Lee, invented the World Wide Web, and no-one could have foreseen the massive impact it would have on all our lives [15].

It was a time of change for the world and for me too. My destination was Manchester.

I had rather liked the academics I had met from UMIST in the lift in Brussels. Their Department of Computation had a bias towards the practical application and use of computers that greatly appealed to me. I felt I would fit in well and it would be worth the sixty-mile round trip each day.

At my interview there, I was offered a post as Lecturer. I saw this as a step backwards in my career, for I'd hoped to be appointed Senior Lecturer straight away, being equivalent to my current position. I was especially disappointed because recently I had been awarded a major research grant and would be taking that with me. They assured me that with a few more journal publications I would soon be promoted.

From the outset I decided not to mention that I had children. This made me rather sad, but I wanted to be taken seriously for my research. The department was male-dominated and to most of them women were wives, mothers or secretaries but rarely academic colleagues. Studies have since backed up my theory that a 'motherhood penalty' exists [8] with an assumption that women with children are not fully focussed on their work, will need more days off or will leave work early, whereas men with children are thought to be more reliable, steady and worthy of promotion. Recent evidence also shows that, for most men, fatherhood results in a wage bonus, whereas

[44] https://en.wikipedia.org/wiki/Poll_tax_riots

for most women, motherhood results in a wage penalty [16]. I just wanted to be accepted for myself and what I was capable of professionally and not to have my destiny dictated by other people's preconceptions of wives and mothers.

Joining a research group was an expectation of the department. I was courted by Prof Singh, Head of the Decision Sciences[45] group; he was shrewd and skilful in achieving what he wanted. I thought, 'Why not? I might learn something.' I joined in 1990, wearing a suit with shoulder pads and a slightly above-the-knee skirt, and felt flattered when he said I was a young woman with my future ahead of me. At 40, with three children, I didn't feel that young, but his confidence put a smile on my face and gave me a real boost. Aside from me, his group consisted of two academics, two secretaries, a programmer and a number of doctoral students.

Prof Singh was a charismatic, persuasive person who would impress visitors with his international awards and plaques strategically placed throughout his large office. He developed techniques for practical decision-making and at the time worked with companies who supplied petrol on the forecourts.

His software analysed a range of data based on factors such as location and volume of sales and also soft data relating to management goals. The software would calculate an optimum price to charge for petrol at the pumps. At that time all petrol from the same company, such as ESSO, would be the same price wherever it was sold. Prof Singh's algorithms would enable local pricing of petrol which in the long term proved to

[45] Decision Sciences help executives make strategic decisions using modelling and prediction based on everyday information, qualitative and quantitative data.

be very popular (and profitable). He was so confident in his work that he would tell clients they could have his software free of charge but in exchange he wanted 1% of the attributable profits made in the first three years.

He had mastered a virtuous cycle. He developed the techniques based on theory, tried them out in a real-life situation and then dictated a paper for one of his secretaries to type, format, review and submit to a journal for publication. He grew a formidable research reputation as well as a successful business. I was impressed by the cycle of theory - new technique - application - publication and business growth - then back into theory. Prof S was indeed a clever man!

One of the first things he said to me on joining his group was, "If anyone asks you to do anything, don't answer until you have asked yourself, 'What's in it for me?'"

To some people this may seem obvious, but I was quite shocked. 'What's in it for me?' Surely, it was not just about me; how would my decision affect others? Was it the right thing to do? It seemed terribly selfish. Mum had taught us to be kind, consider the other person and try to do good in the world.

At the same time, I could see that this was probably why he was so successful. Every action, every decision was calculated, weighed up and negotiated until he found the advantage for himself.

Shortly after joining, I was called into the head of department's office, along with the one other female academic. She was younger than me, had a bohemian style and wore loose, colourful clothing. He was a tall, imposing man, a hardware engineer with a command-and-control leadership style and a Northern accent.

"Na then, girls," he said. "Why aren't there more girls in the department? How do we recruit more?"

He pointed to the fact that only ten per cent of undergraduates were women, though clearly, he had failed to notice that only five per cent of his academic staff were female.

I was rather taken aback by his question. What was I supposed to do about it? I found the predominantly male environment rather aggressive, and he was almost blaming us for not recruiting more 'girls', when in my mind it was clearly the fault of the 'boys'.

There were around 40 academic staff with only two women, me and Dr Alison Adam. Her research domain was Feminism and Artificial Intelligence [17]. The men often confused us, calling me Alison and calling her Linda. We did not look alike or dress alike, but I guess a woman is a woman if you're a man, they're all the same after all. The head of department just wanted more! And apparently it was our responsibility to recruit them.

'Aha,' I thought. 'What's in it for me?' (I'm a quick learner).

Why should I spend my time trying to recruit more female students while the men were busy doing their research? I knew it would mean being rolled out at every student open day: 'Look, we have a woman – just like you' and doing more than my fair share of recruitment. Of course, I would do my bit just as much as the men did. In any case, might not a handsome young male lecturer be more successful at attracting the girls?

We made agreeable noises to the Head, but he hadn't set us any specific objectives, so it seemed safe not to do anything. Alison was slightly more enthusiastic than me, much more in touch with the issues and a member of WISE (Women into Science and Technology)[46].

---

[46] WISE -Women into Science and Technology was founded in 1984 to encourage more women into Engineering https://www.wisecampaign.org.uk/history/

Aware of the constant fight to find time to do research, I had to be strict with myself about saying 'yes'. It is now well documented that 'women are asked to do more undervalued admin work than their male colleagues - and they say yes because they are penalised for being unlikeable if they say no' [18] (p. 98).
Often male colleagues would feign incompetence at admin or deliberately not do the work until it was taken from them.

I'd arrived at UMIST with strong links with industry, a private consultancy and a major research grant. Human Computer Interaction continued to be the focus of my research but with the emphasis shifting to the early stages of the software development process. Experience in the NHS had taught me that it was no use starting to write a computer program until you understood what the user really needed.

In essence, the first stage of software development is requirements capture - finding out about the users and their goals; the next stage is design - describing and modelling the system: inputs, processes, outputs; next, a more detailed user-interface design and a specification of the programs that need to be written; finally, the programming or coding itself. Not forgetting testing …

Much of my Human Computer Interaction research to date focussed on user-interface design and it was my contention that, to find the right match between the system design and user needs, we must encourage designers to focus on users from the outset.

My mission as a researcher was to develop techniques that would enable designers to think about users and to follow that human-centred design through to the coding stage. All too often, users were forgotten when it came to the technical programming, leading to software that was difficult to use or didn't fit in with the tasks they wanted to carry out. I'd been working on these techniques for a while, incorporating them into my teaching of undergraduates and later publishing them in a book called 'Human Computer Interaction for Software Designers' [19].

The consultancy with International Computers Ltd (ICL) gave me insights into how the specification of new software products was reached. It also provided the opportunity to influence product teams' understanding of users at the requirements capture stage.

Typically, teams would be from different backgrounds and have differing opinions about what was needed, often making it difficult to reach agreement. They might be marketeers, designers, software engineers, technical authors or project managers and often needed the services of a professional facilitator to help them arrive at timely decisions.

My own experience has taught me that a professional meetings facilitator is a highly skilled job where he or she is constantly picking up cues from participants: what they are saying; who they are looking at; friendly or hostile attitudes; disagreements; levels of participation and many more, while at the same time guiding the group to a meaningful outcome.

The major research grant I'd brought with me to UMIST was called 'Co-operative Requirements Capture',[47] the overall aims being to build computer support for the facilitator and the team, and automatically document the agreed user-centred requirements [20].

Videoconferencing tools were in their infancy at the time and offered only a basic level of communication. We found video interaction unreliable and decided to ignore it completely, instead setting up a software platform[48] that enabled both group-wide textual communication and private one-to-one conversation. The software monitored and analysed every exchange, both shared and private, and derived patterns of behaviour that would be useful to the facilitator.

Avatars mimicking individual behaviours based on textual exchanges

[47] It was worth almost half a million pounds over a period of three years, jointly funded by the Science and Engineering Research Council, the Government's Department of Trade and Industry and ICL.

[48] We designed the platform on SUN Workstations using CLOS: The Common Lisp Object system

For example, one of the meeting problem syndromes described earlier is the 'dominant species' syndrome, where one or two people dominate the discussion and others get frustrated or withdraw because they are not heard.

The question is: how does the facilitator know this problem is developing when she/he can't see or hear them?

With the software she/he can see a number of windows on a large screen. In one window she/he can see human-like images (avatars) seated around a table. Each avatar represents one group member and mimics that person's behaviour.

The more active a member is the closer the avatar moves towards the table, the less active it moves further away. If a member isn't active for a while the avatar will lean back in the chair and 'zzzzzz' will appear over its head, i.e. it would start snoring. If two members are arguing, their avatars will move closer in towards each other.

The facilitator watches the avatar behaviour on screen, while at the same time another window shows a bar-chart-style analysis of the levels of participation of each member. They also follow the textual exchanges to ascertain whether the conversation is on track and intervening if problems are arising. One intervention in the case of the 'dominant species' syndrome would be to do a 'round robin': to get each person to say something and limit their contribution time.

The professional facilitator is not a member of the team and consequently not necessarily knowledgeable about the technical content of the conversation. To assist with this the software analyses the actual words used by participants and produces a mapping of frequently used words against time.

Experiments were conducted over a Local Area Network: each team member was in a different room, as was the facilitator. After trialling our software, we brought in professional requirements teams from our industry collaborators to test whether they felt it would work in practice.

Our business partners were quite excited by the potential of this approach and especially liked the idea that ultimately the software might allow one facilitator to run several (remote) group meetings simultaneously [21].

I didn't quite achieve the virtuous cycle of Prof Singh but was definitely heading in the right direction. My HCI research [19] contributed to the development of techniques used in the Marketing to Design workshops. The experience of applying the techniques enabled me to write up a theory-into-practice journal paper. The problems encountered and insights gained formed the foundation of future research grant applications.

Although it was lovely to be paid generously for consultancy and bring real value to companies, I had no interest in running or owning a business myself. My overall goal was to keep learning about the role of technology in supporting person-to-person interaction and the new opportunities that it might provide.

Despite the setback in changing jobs, it wasn't long before I was feeling settled. In this new environment I had to reassess my strengths and weaknesses and set myself new goals. I already had a strong research agenda, a track record of research grants and high-quality international conference and journal papers. My main weaknesses were the lack of publications in the highest-ranking journals and the fact that I didn't have a PhD.

I set myself short-term and long-term goals: within three years to get my PhD and be promoted to senior lecturer (SL) and within seven to professor. I ascertained the criteria for promotion to SL and set myself rolling twelve-month objectives to achieve them. The criteria for a professorship were rather more elusive. "You know when someone is ready" was the type of comment made. I would have to study those who had been recently promoted and make my own list.

One approach to achieving a higher standard in journal papers is to first publish the research in a conference. An international conference where papers are fully refereed and have a low acceptance rate will usually provide good quality feedback. The research can then be further developed and reported in a journal paper.

I had such a paper [22] accepted at the IEEE[49] First International Conference on Requirements Engineering. It was to be held in San Diego, California. I was excited to go, never having been across the Atlantic. I travelled alone via Heathrow, confident but apprehensive about finding my way around. The conference was held in January 1993 at the historic beachside Hotel del Coronado, the glamorous location of the 1959 film 'Some Like it Hot' starring Marilyn Monroe. It hardly ever rains in San Diego but sure enough it did rain when I was there! Did I take the Manchester weather with me?

Looking down the attendance list, I identified a number of people I wanted to meet. I would go to their presentations, ask questions and speak to them afterwards. I would also see which sessions they attended and, if possible, go to those too. It was important that I got to know their work and that they got to know mine, so I tried to be active and make the most of the opportunity to meet well-known researchers from across the world.

Often (predominantly male) attendees would go to the bar after the day's sessions, discuss research and just get to know each other informally. I would join them at first but, once they'd had a drink or two, I would make my excuse and leave. They would plan to go into the city and enjoy the nightlife, but it didn't seem appropriate for me to join them. I missed out on the camaraderie between the men with their informal plotting and manoeuvring. I wasn't 'one of the lads' and whilst at the conference had heard the way some of them spoke about the women.

---

[49] IEEE Institute of Electrical and Electronic Engineering, https://ieeexplore.ieee.org/Xplore/home.jsp

Despite that, one thoughtful colleague, at the conference with his wife and children, kindly asked if I would like to accompany them on a day trip to Tijuana on the Mexican border – a short 15-mile drive from San Diego but a totally different world. As we approached the border, we saw people living in cars – dozens of them along both sides of the road – who were clearly in need, and the sight made me feel uncomfortable. We had to transfer from the car into a coach to cross the border and travel into Tijuana. Its bustling main street, Avenida Revolucion, was lined with souvenir shops, lively bars with flashing neon signs and stalls selling leather goods. My colleague helped me negotiate for a cowboy-style leather saddlebag to take home for Patrick. I knew he would love it. Tijuana was quite an experience, a bit scary, but exciting. Nonetheless I was glad to get back to the hotel.

By the end of the conference, I'd had some excellent feedback and felt I was becoming established as someone doing leading-edge research in the field of Requirements Engineering. I travelled home feeling quite pleased.

I was happy to be home and see the children for what was left of the school holidays. Theresa and Christine were aged 9 and 8 by this time and still at junior school whilst Jon, now 17, was at college. I'd felt only slightly guilty about leaving them because they were all very encouraging and happy to wave me off. In any case they had the best dad ever and I knew they would be fine.

My mother encouraged me too and, although my world was very different from hers, she knew about people and their ways and would sometimes mentor me on how to deal with difficult situations. She was my role model too, a strong independent woman who, despite life's setbacks, always found a way to be positive and kind to others.

Mum continued to provide a safe haven for the girls before and after school and occasionally she would come out with us.

One weekend, while we were at the Lightwater Valley Theme Park in North Yorkshire, she complained of a headache and dots before her eyes. She was worried that she might be losing her sight and, despite numerous doctors' appointments, it seemed that nothing could be done.

One Saturday, when Christine and I took sandwiches to Mum's to have lunch together, we found her on the bathroom floor complaining of a terrible headache and sickness. I called our GP who came around within the hour and said she had food poisoning and should rest.

Eventually, I got her into bed and she seemed to be asleep when I left her at 9 pm. I worried all night and, early next morning, went to see her only to find her on the floor again. I called our next-door neighbour, a staff nurse, who came at once, took one look at her and said, "She's had a stroke; ring for an ambulance".

Mum was barely conscious when she reached the hospital and died two days later. If only I had called an ambulance earlier, but I had no idea what a stroke looked like and I had trusted the GP. My two sisters travelled up from London and Cambridge and arrived just in time to say their farewells. My brother arrived later; he was working offshore on an oil rig and had to be helicoptered in. He couldn't believe that Mum was dead. "Just let me see her, hold her hand and everything will be all right." He did hold her hand and was stunned; everything was not 'going to be all right'.

I couldn't go into work; it was the middle of term and I had to get someone to notify my students. I called a close colleague to tell him what needed to be done and to ask for help. I thought I was strong but, when I started speaking, I completely broke down. It was so hard to say, "Mum is dead". Fortunately, Jon, then 18, stepped in, took the phone from me and sorted everything out.

Mum was so loved that over a hundred people came to her funeral service in Halifax, and then a long entourage of cars followed us to Burnley Cemetery where she was to be buried next to Dad. Many more people turned up at the cemetery; her friends from Burnley had spread the word. We were heartened and delighted by the outpouring of love for her.

She left four children, twelve grandchildren and two great-grandchildren when she died at the age of 68, and a total of £7 in the bank.

I'd lost my friend, my confidante, my mentor and role model. For years after I would see her in the street or walking through the park near our house. Sometimes she visits me in my dreams; I can see her. She will never leave me.

Having lived through the Second World War, my mother would have seen the growing importance of technology in communication. The telegraph, the radio and telephone all played a part in her life. She had used a comptometer and an electric typewriter at work and seen her grandchildren play rudimentary computer games, but she would have been unprepared for the unprecedented integration of the computer and communications worlds that was about to happen.

The internet was growing apace. Nothing would ever be the same again.

Chapter 10 The internet and the world wide web

Laying internet cables under the sea

Grieving is a slow process; when my Dad died it took five years before I really felt 'normal' again. Why now? Why did Mum have to go?

Everything seemed much harder after Mum died. A typical weekday consisted of leaving home at about 7 am to start the thirty-mile journey to work. I'd walk to the station, take the train to Manchester then walk across the city, taking about an hour and a half on a good day, be busy all day then return home exhausted at about 7 pm. Why didn't we move to Manchester, you might ask? Patrick's work was about six miles in the opposite direction to mine, the children were settled in school and we had a lovely big house and garden, so it seemed right to stay where we were. I could look for a job nearer to home but then it wouldn't be the job that I wanted. What's more I owed it to Mum to make the most of the opportunities and motivation she had given me. I only wish life had been kinder to her. Her children all had good careers and her daughters were more than capable of being financially independent, which was what she wanted. I just had to 'get on with it'; the world was changing, and I had to change with it.

We managed to get help on weekdays through a friend of a friend who came in the afternoons, did a little cleaning and prepared the evening meal. At one point I felt that my weekends were made up entirely of washing and ironing and thought to myself: 'is this really how I want to spend my life?' Eventually I found another lovely lady to take a basket of laundry on Saturday and bring it back, beautifully ironed, on Sunday evening – she made me so happy.

It was clear that the internet was going to bring new and exciting challenges to my research, and I wanted to engage. I'd achieved my promotion to senior lecturer but was behind with my plan for a professorship. In the mid-1990s the internet was mainly used by scientists and academics, most computers still used floppy disks and were connected to the internet via dial-up modems[50]. It is estimated that only 10,000 websites existed worldwide[51], so the majority of people had never experienced it.

The internet itself is a worldwide physical infrastructure that allows computer networks, run by companies, governments, universities and other organisations, to connect to each other. It is a mass of cables, computers, datacentres, routers, servers and satellites which allows information to travel around the world.[52] Hundreds of thousands of miles of cable criss-cross countries and are laid along seabeds to connect islands and

---

[50] A modem modulates and demodulates electrical signals - it transforms digital information from a computer into analogue signals that can transmit over wires and translates incoming analogue signals back into digital data

[51]https://www.syracuse.com/news/2014/11/technology_history_internet_computers_phones_1994.html
1994 in technology: What the Internet, computers and phones were like 20 years ago,
by Geoff Herbert, 22 March 2019, accessed 15/03/2020

[52]https://www.theguardian.com/technology/2018/oct/22/what-is-the-internet-13-key-questions-answered, What is the Internet by Ian Sample, Science Editor, 22 October 2018, accessed 17/03/2020

continents. For example, cables under the Pacific Ocean link California to Singapore and Hong Kong[53].

The Manchester Evening News (MEN) were keen to explore the potential of the internet for their newspaper and in the mid-1990s asked me to experiment with alternative designs for internet delivery. Some of the paper's senior staff were against change and couldn't see the value of the internet, so part of the project was to show them what could be done. At that time a newspaper's identity was defined by the layout of the printed page and the sequence of pages: news, local articles, classified ads, business, sport.

My research group created two websites, one of which maintained the layout of the newspaper where articles could be found by scrolling and another, newly designed to take account of the small screen size and make links between screens. We recruited users, mainly from staff, students, and ex-students, to help with evaluation. Many overseas students had loved to read the reports of the Manchester football teams and had the paper posted to them after leaving university. They were delighted to see it online. The vast majority preferred the new design but, in many ways, it didn't really matter what the result of the evaluation was; when we presented our findings to MEN staff they were just amazed by the number of international readers from as far afield as China, Malaysia, India and Greece. The thought that their 'local' paper could be read across the world was enough to convince them to take the next step[54].

I quite enjoyed giving presentations, especially to businesspeople and I'd had plenty of practice. Nonetheless, as part of my staff training, I opted to go on a two-day course in

[53] The cable is over 12,000 miles long and went into service in 2009 (the Asia-America Gateway)

[54] It was a big step, although leading the field it wasn't until 1998 that the Manchester Evening News went online

London to hone my skills. The organisers told us to throw away our PowerPoint slides and speak from the heart, using only sketches we'd created ourselves. Our presentations were videoed, and feedback given in front of the group. When I got home my teenage daughters asked," What did you do on the course, Mum?"

"I was learning how to improve my presentation skills; I was recorded on video. Do you want to have a look?"

"Oh, yes please," they said, eagerly.

I showed them the video and they both looked really disappointed.

"Huh, you mean you get paid for doing THAT!"

They looked at each other as if to say, 'we could easily do that.' I didn't know whether to be pleased or not.

By now MEN staff were using the internet, that is, the physical computer networks; the actual content of the newspaper was delivered via the World Wide Web. The web allows any person to share information with anyone else, no matter where they are, and without having to think about the physical route it takes across the internet.

The fact that anyone could share anything gave the web a feeling of the Wild West, where there were no rules, no ethics, no sense of morality, no standards of behaviour, no penalties. At first it didn't feel like a very safe place. A parallel world was being created and the politicians and police were way behind. There were mixed feelings as to whether it held promise for women, which was a topic for discussion at the 1997 Women in Computing conference – 'on the one hand the more communicative character of the internet might be better adapted to women's needs. On the other, pornography and aggressive interaction styles might deter women from using it'. [23]

The World Wide Web Consortium(W3C)[55], founded in 1994, upholds egalitarian principles vital to the future of the web, but those principles are more about equality of access and technical standards rather than the behaviour of people. There are four important principles: universality, open and royalty-free access, net neutrality and decentralisation.

Universality: allowing people to put anything on the web, no matter what computer they have, software they use or human language they speak

Open and royalty free access to the technical standards on which the web operates: allowing people to create applications without anyone's permission or having to pay

Net neutrality: allowing all internet communications to be treated equally regardless of source or content and that internet service providers may not intentionally block, slow down or charge money for specific services.

Decentralisation: the web has no 'centre', its large collection of hypertext, graphics, sound, video and other information sources reside on thousands of computers connected to the internet. No approval is needed to add a web page or make a link.

The creation of W3C gave some reassurance that the web wasn't going to be taken over by one of the big computer companies or by an alien power. The consortium is made up of people from business, governments and universities who are dedicated to upholding these egalitarian principles and developing protocols and guidelines, so that everyone in the world can benefit. [24]

My main interest was in how the web could be used by business and its impact on human computer interaction. The

---

[55] Tim Berners-Lee, a British scientist who created the first website and browser in 1989, is both a visionary and an ardent defender of the world wide web, also founder and director of the World Wide Web Consortium (W3C)

MEN experience was just the start; I decided to reach out to local businesses and organised a number of evening sessions to raise their awareness of what was possible and to build a network where businesses could share knowledge and expertise with each other as well as myself and my research team. We were able to leverage funding to work with smaller businesses to get them up and running on the internet and into e-commerce. For example, in the late 1990s a company called Cooksons who sold DIY products to tradespeople via a physical shop counter wanted to make them available online for purchase by the general public. Funding from the DTI[56] paid for a full-time programmer to work in the company and the EPSRC[57] paid me to manage and direct the project half a day a week.

The owner's dream was to get away from the old warehouse in Stockport and be able to run the business from his yacht in the Mediterranean. We worked with him for two years designing, building and testing his website, pioneering e-commerce capability and educating his staff how to run the site. The e-commerce site was eventually extended to full e-business, that is, not just selling online but also automating business processes such as stock control, warehousing, order fulfilment and customer support. It took five years to achieve his dream; ultimately, he carried out customer support and actually ran his business by satellite, internet and phone from his yacht. I can picture him now on a sun lounger, floating in the gentle Mediterranean Sea, glass in one hand, satellite phone in the

[56] DTI is The Department of Trade and Industry, a UK government department formed on 19 October 1970.

[57] EPSRC is The Engineering and Physical Sciences Research Council (EPSRC) is the main funding body for engineering and physical sciences research in the UK. https://epsrc.ukri.org

other, soothing the irate customer from rainy Stockport demanding to know where his garden gravel is.

I loved being involved with real businesses because it was here that you saw the richness of life, where everything is interconnected. It was vital to carry out the technical design and programming correctly, focus on the human computer interaction design to be sure people could use it and maintain it, and think about how people's jobs and organisations would change, along with the future potential for the business. A truly holistic view was needed together with an opportunity to put theory into practice.

One Monday morning, my walk into work was disrupted by the aftermath of a massive bomb explosion in Manchester city centre - Saturday 15th June 1996. The Irish Republican Army (IRA) had detonated the biggest bomb seen in Britain since the Second World War. A lorry containing 1,500kg of explosives was driven into the Arndale Centre on Corporation Street and detonated. It was very upsetting, though miraculously, no-one was killed. The IRA claimed responsibility, they even called the police with a prior warning, but no-one was ever charged. The city centre was out of bounds for quite some time while the rubble was cleared, buildings made safe and a massive regeneration programme undertaken.

My walking route across Manchester was now dirty, dusty and generally unpleasant, so I decided to come into work by car. Patrick kindly agreed to take the bus.

I managed to organise my timetable so that most weeks I could work at home for two days. It was much easier to focus, write research papers, reports and grant proposals and, of course, catch up with my marking. By 1996 I'd published around fourteen journal papers and, with my doctoral students, had presented our work at around twenty international conferences. I'd been at UMIST for seven years and was granted a twelve-months' sabbatical to write up my own doctoral thesis called:

'The Role of the Facilitator in Distributed Teamwork' [25]. Additionally, I was keen to communicate my understanding of the tools and techniques needed for the early stages of the requirements process, and authored a book: 'Requirements Engineering' with Springer Applied Computing series. [26]

Partway through my sabbatical, I met a number of like-minded researchers at the IEEE Conference on Requirements Engineering held in Colorado Springs, USA [27], literally a breath-taking place with an elevation of over 6,000ft on the eastern foot of the Rocky Mountains. I felt at ease at the conference, despite the small number of women presenters. Those women who were there were exceptional and doing research that complemented my own.

In 1997 I was pleased to have a paper accepted at the International Conference on Human Computer Interaction in San Francisco, USA [28] and to have a further opportunity to network with researchers from across the world. The conference was held in August, in the middle of the school holidays, so we decided to combine it with a family holiday. By this time Theresa and Christine were mid-teens and Jon was at university. Jon was running his own entertainments security business in his spare time and decided he was too busy to come.

The four of us went away for three weeks. The first week I would attend the conference while Patrick and the girls explored San Francisco. The second week we would drive to Yosemite National Park, then return to San Francisco and fly to New York for the third week.

The conference was held in the San Francisco Hilton, quite luxurious for us thinking back to our hitch-hiking days or wet camping holidays in England. We upgraded my single room, booked by the university, to a family suite with two double beds. Patrick took the girls sightseeing during the day, while I attended the conference and continued to build my research network. It was a large conference of around six hundred attendees, so I had to select carefully which sessions to attend and who I wanted to meet. It was, generally, a female-friendly conference, as are most with the word 'human' in the title.

There was so much to see: Fisherman's Wharf, San Francisco Museum of Modern Art, trams, Sears store, Haight-Ashbury, the view from Coit Tower and the ferry to Sausalito. I joined them for the last few days, we hired a car and drove down Lombard Street and across the Golden Gate bridge. This was Patrick's first time in America, and he was a little apprehensive about driving an automatic car and on the right-hand side of the road. He soon mastered it and at the end of the week we set off to Yosemite.

It was quite a shock for us when we arrived at Yosemite; we had booked a 'canvas cabin' in the park itself and when we located it my first reaction was, 'Oh no, we can't possibly stay here; there must be a mistake'. We went back to the reception desk to check, but yes that was it. The 'canvas cabin' was literally that: a wooden frame with canvas over the top and sides, and a wood door. There was no sink, no toilet, no stove, no heater, no cupboards, nowhere to hang clothes, just two iron-framed beds with thin mattresses and a bare light bulb. The contrast with our en-suite room at the Hilton was stark. But that was it, no alternative! Was I getting soft? Why wasn't I more grateful to have any kind of accommodation in such an amazing setting.

We had been warned about bears roaming around the park at night. 'Do not leave food in your car. Lock toothpaste, cosmetics, toiletries in the lockers provided. Do not eat in the cabins.' We had been there a few days, saw no sign of a bear and so were beginning to think it was just something they told tourists. We had to eat at the cafes in the park and they all closed at sunset. Once it was dark there wasn't much you could do but go back to the cabin and go to bed. One night, when the girls were fast asleep and I was sitting up in bed trying to read, Patrick went out to the shower block to go to the toilet. He seemed to take a long time and I was just getting really worried about him when he burst through the door, shut it behind him and, breathing heavily, stood with his back against it.

"I've just seen a bear." His face was as white as a sheet.

"I was walking to the shower block and suddenly it appeared in front of me and rose up onto its hind legs; it was ten feet tall." We'd been told to make a loud noise if confronted with a bear and it would back off.

"I just ran as fast as I could into the block, went into a cubicle, locked the door and stood on the toilet seat so that he couldn't see me below the door." He was still out of breath; he'd had a terrible fright and felt he had to run for his life.

"I waited and waited until I thought the bear had gone, slowly looked out and then ran as fast as I could back to the cabin."

He took a while to calm down, but then we had a good laugh, though not too loud, in case the bears heard us.

Every night after that we could hear their footsteps and low growling as they roamed round seemingly very close to our thin canvas walls. They were looking for food. Now we understood the warnings about not bringing food into the cabin or car and were super-conscientious from then on.

Yosemite itself is a huge tranquil place with rivers, waterfalls, mountains, meadows, giant sequoia trees, a vast wilderness of the kind you cannot see in Britain: a privilege to be so close to nature with wonderful plants and trees and to walk the pathways freely. The girls swam in the crystal-clear ice-cold rivers and we all relaxed away from the stresses of the city.

The week under canvas over, we headed back to San Francisco and on to New York. We walked and took the subway to get a feel for the city, visited St. Patrick's Cathedral, saw Times Square at night and rode in the elevator 110 floors to the top of one of the Twin Towers, experiencing a breath-taking view across the city (and a rather scary one if you ventured towards the perimeter), its roof being over a quarter of a mile high.

On our last day, everyone was in a state of shock when we woke to the news that Princess Diana[58] had been killed in a car crash. It was headline news on the TV in the hotel and on the front page of every newspaper in New York.

We flew home to a grieving nation, flags at half-mast and a million floral tributes laid outside Buckingham Palace. Women seemed to be particularly affected[59], for many identified with Diana's kindness and the vulnerability she had spoken of in the years and months before her death [29]. She was a mother of two young boys and, despite being a 'royal', had an extraordinary ability to identify with 'ordinary' people. Her funeral was watched by over 2.5 billion people worldwide and it was impossible not to be saddened by her death.

Once back to work, it was time to take stock and devise a plan for getting a professorship. I'd been busy for a while working out how to get promotion and building my profile accordingly. In the absence of any formal document, I put together some criteria based on information gleaned. That statement "You know when someone is ready," really wasn't a great help!

Criteria included: £1million in external funding, research papers published in top journals, an international reputation for the quality of your research, leadership in the form of your own research group, future potential for growth, citizenship within the university and externally, an offer of a chair from another

[58] Diana, Princess of Wales (born Diana Frances Spencer; 1 July 1961 – 31 August 1997) was a member of the British royal family. She was the first wife of Charles, Prince of Wales, and the mother of Prince William and Prince Harry.

[59] Later research showed that suicide and self-harm among women age 25-40 rose by 45% in the months after her death [29].

university of a similar standing or a Nobel Prize or Fellowship of the Royal Society or other outstanding recognition of your work.

Quite a list!

It wasn't just the criteria that mattered; you had to get people on your side. You needed: a friendly professor to help prepare your case; the head of department to approve it being put forward; an external referee to peruse it and agree that there is a 'prima facie' case worthy of putting together an interview panel. In addition to a CV, my case was to include references from twelve external referees of whom six should be internationally recognised researchers in the field. The interview panel itself would consist of a pro-vice-chancellor, all the professors in your department and one external professor, a specialist who could speak about the quality of your published work.

Generally, it was considered harder to obtain a promotional chair[60] within your own university than it was to get a chair at another university.

Additionally, in 1997, across all subject areas in UK universities only 9% of professors were women[61].

In my department all the professors were men and in its thirty-year history not a single woman had been appointed.

I was looking forward to the challenge!

---

[60] 'chair' is used interchangeably with 'professorship'

[61] Higher education employment data – Academic staff 1995 to 2005, UCU University College Union https://www.ucu.org.uk/media/2359/Higher-education-employment-data-academic-staff-Nov-07/pdf/hedata_academicstaff.pdf accessed 7/3/20

Chapter 11 First female professor

Driving into work, I was excited to see billboards advertising a company's website address. I would hurry to look it up and see that it was a static web page, a kind of online brochure. It was early days but, moving apace, businesses were eager to learn, experimenting with reaching out to customers on the internet. 1998 saw the launch of the International Space Station and was a time of great optimism and excitement about new technologies. A small but growing number of UK households were online and the first Wi-Fi was installed in people's homes.[62] Search engines such as Google[63] came on stream, making it easier to find your way around the growing web of information.

The internet and World Wide Web brought new challenges for my research. No longer could we assume that the computer user belonged to an organisation, sitting at a company workstation doing pre-defined tasks. The new users had discretion, used their own computer at home, and were free to choose what to do, to browse, search or purchase products. Users were now potential customers. My field of Human

[62] The number of households online rose from 9% in 1998 to 19% by the year 2000[62] and the first Wi-Fi in UK homes. Computerhistory.org

[63] Google was launched in September 1998

Computer Interaction that lay at the intersection of technological design and behavioural science would now have to be extended to include consumer behaviour.

I was interested in how consumer behaviour would inform the design of e-commerce systems, and joined up with experts in retail marketing, Professor Peter McGoldrick, Professor of Retailing and Dr Kathy Keeling, at Manchester Business School to investigate. We bid for research funding from the Engineering and Physical Sciences Research Council and were successful in winning a major award. The project name: Human Factors in the Design of Electronic Service Delivery Systems for use in Complex Environments.

In addition, I attracted a quarter of a million pounds from the European Regional Development Fund to create a Centre of Expertise in e-commerce to facilitate sharing of research and practice between the university and businesses in the region. The centre hosted a conference in November 1999, and we developed a new master's degree programme in e-commerce to launch the following year.

I was really enjoying work and was excited by the growing number of opportunities for research and engagement with business. Nonetheless, I had to keep a watching eye on my case for promotion; had I been a man it might have been a natural progression, but I wasn't, so I had to try that much harder. With only 9% of professors in any discipline in the UK being women, and none at all in my own department, barriers lay ahead, however good I was (or thought I was).

A relatively recent investigation into women leaders in academia in science and technology illustrated 'the effect of organisational influences such as temporary work arrangements, male-dominated networks, intimidation and harassment, as well as individual influences such as lack of confidence' [30] as barriers to women's progression. The overall picture[64] was improving nationally, reaching 11% in 1999-2000[65], but female professors in computer science, maths and physical sciences lagged behind [31].

If I'd looked at the statistics I might have given up but fortunately, at the time, I was just interested in getting to the next stage in my career. Being a professor would open doors to new opportunities, give me a seat at the decision-making table and enable me to have a wider leadership role.

It wasn't exactly an even playing field; I'd seen two colleagues promoted to chairs and noted the important role their 'stay-at-home' wives played. Apart from looking after the children, they helped with organisational tasks, acted in secretarial roles such as filing documents, photocopying, or assisted with conference organisation, manning the reception desk or meeting and greeting. All of this was lovely, supporting their husbands in a friendly and positive way and enabling them to work more effectively. Could I ask Patrick to come in and do a few jobs for me? That might just be stretching his husbandly duties a bit too far. At times it felt that my colleagues had one-and-a-half people doing their job, compared to my one.

Then there was the dinner party: professors and aspiring professors had dinner parties. Patrick and I had been invited to several friendly 'getting to know you' or 'getting to know your spouse' drinks and canapes occasions with other 'interesting guests' or a delicious meal cooked by the most capable wife and

---

[64] Higher education employment data – Academic staff 1995 to 2005, UCU University College Union https://www.ucu.org.uk/media/2359/Higher-education-employment-data-academic-staff-Nov-07/pdf/hedata_academicstaff.pdf accessed 24/4/2020 page 17

[65] 16% by 2005/6, 25% by 2016/17 https://www.hesa.ac.uk/news/18-01-2018/sfr248-higher-education-staff-statistics
accessed 24/4/2020

hostess. They could just be getting senior colleagues together, but it always felt as if there were another agenda and I usually left feeling indebted to the host in some way. The dinner parties that we weren't invited to were for visiting overseas professors or potential collaborators, very important if you were working with European partners. The social side of research helped build an understanding of each other's language and culture and facilitated better understanding of the research project or funding bid. Would Patrick host a dinner party for me? He was a good cook, his corned beef hash renowned. I decided not to ask.

Aside from doing research and teaching and preparing my CV for promotion, I needed to select and prepare my referees. Because of the applied nature of my research it was agreed that six would be from industry and the other six internationally known professors: twelve in total. I suggested heads of research groups in three major companies and business leaders from three smaller ones, all of whom I had worked with closely in the preceding years. Of the six professors three were from the United States and three from the UK. Preparation of the referees took me two years. I made a point of meeting each one in person, explaining the promotion criteria, asking if they would act as referee and then, as the time to write their letter of support approached, writing to them indicating specifically which research and which period of time they should comment on. It was important that each referee supported me unambiguously and did not give the interview panel any cause for doubt.

My CV was over thirty pages long, typical of an academic, including assessment of my teaching and administration, though the main emphasis was on research and publication: seventeen international journal papers, thirty refereed conference papers, two single-author books, a doctoral thesis and well over a million pounds in external research funding. I would score high on citizenship and community building and my research had a clear direction and potential for growth and further leadership. It felt positive.

It was known among academics in the wider community that I was looking for promotion, resulting in a number of discussions with heads of department. I was impressed by the ambitious plans of the Computer Science department at Hull University, where I was formally interviewed and offered a professorship. Should I accept? Was it worth uprooting the whole family for the sake of my ambition? I wasn't sure. Fortunately (though much to the annoyance of the head of department at Hull) it did have the effect of expediting the date for my interview at UMIST.

When it came to the interview, I felt like an actor in a play: I knew the plot, the stage setting and the main characters. The problem was that the script had been given to all the actors except for me. Imagine the scene: the Vice Chancellor (VC), five departmental professors, one professor from another university (the External) all seated round the boardroom table in the VC's office. The scene opens with shaking of hands, polite exchanges and offers of tea from the secretary. The plot follows the usual pattern: first, exposition of the facts, the CV, the references; then the tension rises as discussion and differences of opinions build. The object of their discussion (me) enters, the VC welcomes me then passes control to the External. The climax is reached as he cross-examines me on the quality of my research, my knowledge of the wider field, the 'who's who' of my subject, my future research plans and what the key problems are that remain to be solved. All eyes are on me. I wish I had a script. Would my 'ad-lib' be enough?

Let's meet some of the characters. As I look around the table, I'm thinking: will he support my case or not?

Prof A: At meetings he always made a point of brushing past me or sitting too close. I would look him directly in the eyes as if to say, 'just you dare try anything with me'. I found him difficult because he had a preference for female project students, master's dissertations in particular, where he relished the one-to-one tutorial. I was concerned for the students, and although everyone seemed to know 'something was going on', no-one was prepared to talk about it. He was in charge of the departmental stock cupboard and would haggle over a box of paper clips. I never quite forgave him for refusing me a supply of a dozen box files for my new office. Despite all this, I needed him on my side to support my promotion case. Would he support me? He would probably follow the lead of Prof B.

Prof B: I had had a number of successful collaborations with Professor B and felt I'd got to know him fairly well. We worked together on a software maintenance research project [32] that involved visiting several companies near London. We occasionally stayed at his parents' house. I was in awe of his Mum. She made breakfast for everyone, cleared the table, loaded the dishwasher, cleaned all the surfaces and was ready to go out to work with the rest of us at 8am. Such efficiency!

Prof B and I were part of a major project with British Telecom (BT). The internet had potential to cause massive disruption to the software industry, so the project's aim was to investigate the future of software. Keele and Durham universities were also involved [33]. Prof B was interested in the students too and we worked together on a distributed software engineering project across the three universities [34].

He was a natural leader, could see the bigger picture and was thoughtful of others. A man you could trust, who liked 'to get things done', he was incredibly efficient and helped everyone, including me, raise the standard of their work. I joined his research group when he went forward for his own professorship and I like to think I helped him in some small way. I felt fairly confident that he would support my case.

Prof C: he was totally immersed in his own research, not interested in departmental politics, a pleasant, interesting man who kept to himself, looked a bit like Bruce Springsteen and was four years younger than me. He was supportive of my work but on the whole seemed indifferent to most things that distracted him from his studies. He would probably just go with the flow.

Prof D: he was an affable, agreeable person, politically very astute. I'd had a number of research collaborations with him in the field of Requirements Engineering (RE) and was very considerate towards me at my first RE conference in San Diego. He invited me onto the editorial board of the International RE Journal, introduced me to some of his European colleagues in Brussels, Milan and Paris, and we had worked on a couple of joint research proposals. He understood how to manoeuvre to his advantage within Europe. I felt he would probably support my case.

Prof E: he was the charismatic, persuasive man we met earlier, very successful both academically and in business, conscious of his status, proud of his awards and international recognition. He was always charming when I went to see him, but I couldn't help feeling like a fly trapped in a spider's web, stuck on sticky threads trying to escape. He wasn't a man to be crossed and was probably annoyed with me for leaving his research group to join with Prof B. Although, on being asked, he didn't say he wouldn't support my case but then he didn't exactly say he would.

The External: the external professor was chosen by the five departmental professors for his knowledge of my research field. He had been asked to read my published papers, to express an opinion about the quality of research to the panel and to ask me probing questions. The VC especially would look to him for an objective view of my worthiness for promotion. I had met him at conferences and given guest lectures at his university, we got on well and I learnt a lot from him about systems thinking and the value-laden nature of technological design. I felt I understood how he thought and what kind of answers would please him.

Everyone was engrossed in the exchange between the External and me, but at the same time looking at each other as if to weigh up what the other person was thinking. What were they thinking? I wish I knew.

At last, they reached the end of the cross-examination and, still feeling like the main actor in a play, I was asked to leave the room and wait in the secretary's office for the resolution of the drama. I waited and waited, until, at length, Prof B called me into the interview room. The VC said, "Congratulations, Professor Macaulay!". Excellent, such a relief, it was smiles and congratulations all round, the five profs and the External. I was delighted.

The VC had a private word with me at his door while the other profs walked down the corridor back to the department. Just as I was turning to leave the VC, I overheard one of the profs say to another,

"You realise that *her* promotion devalues our position?"

It was a whisper, but a loud whisper that I'm sure he meant me to overhear.

How did I feel, you might ask?

How would you feel?

Shocked, frustrated, hurt, angry?

All of the above? Yes, but then I thought, 'Well that's his problem, not mine! I've been appointed Professor of System Design at the University of Manchester Institute of Science and Technology, the first female professor in the thirty-year history of the Department of Computation,' and I felt quite pleased with myself[66].

I could see that I would need to keep an eye on departmental politics but was more excited by what was going

[66] It was 1999 and I was 50 years old

on in the software industry. We felt a sense of trepidation at the approach of the new millennium.

Chapter 12 The heady days of e-commerce

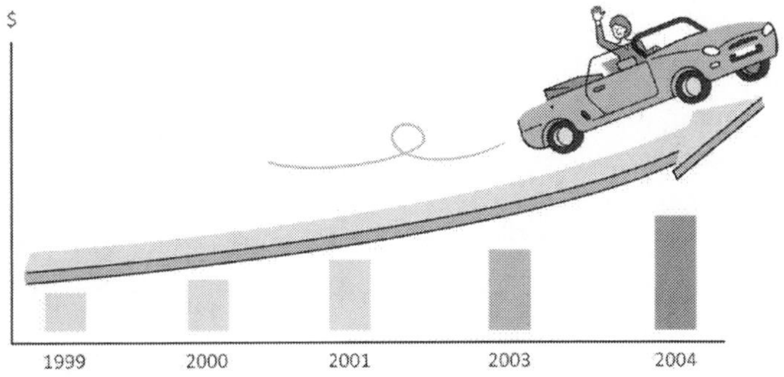

New Year's Eve 1999, the start of a new millennium, gave rise to so much hope and excitement as countries around the world celebrated the end of the 1900s and the beginning of the 2000s. At the stroke of midnight, fireworks were timed to go off, and those countries close to the International Date Line, such as New Zealand, Tonga and Fiji, vied for position to be the first to enter the new millennium.

We were in Halifax, England, hosting a party for our friends and neighbours. We had log fires and candles burning in our basement rooms and the whole house was decorated for Christmas and New Year. My favourite room was the lounge, where the coal fire gave out a warm festive glow and the television was on. Would aeroplanes fall from the sky as predicted? No-one else seemed to be worried, just me. I kept popping in to look at the TV for reports of the impact of the millennium bug[67] but none came; Sydney, Tokyo, Beijing, Moscow and Paris all passed midnight without a single incident.

The millennium bug was caused by programmers in the 1960s to 1980s trying to save expensive memory space by using

[67] Also referred to as the Y2K problem

only two digits to represent the date. For example, the date 1998 was simply '98', 1999 was '99' and 1900 was '00', indistinguishable from 2000 which was also '00'. On calculating your tax bill for the year 'Apr 1999 to Apr 2000' the computer might interpret it as 'Apr 1999 to Apr 1900' and result in a bill for minus 99 years. In other words, any computer that depended on the date in any calculation may get it wrong.

I was worried because I was one of those programmers, and at the time had no idea that software written in the 1970s would still be used in the year 2000. Some of our collaborators were worried too, one even stockpiling food fearing that the worst-case scenario might actually happen. In the event, very few failures were reported; companies had invested heavily in fixing the problem and attaining the 1997 British Standards Institute 'Y2K Conformity Requirements'. Nonetheless it was a stark reminder of the legacy of old computer programmes and the need to future-proof.

One advantage of this was that it forced companies to audit and test their software and, where necessary, to replace it with new code. All of this meant that businesses were in better shape to incorporate the new internet-based applications into their systems.

I remember being very happy in the year 2000 because Patrick had bought me an MGF convertible sports car for my birthday and every day I positively looked forward to the drive to and from work. The car fitted like a glove, with the engine at the rear and my seat warm even in the cold winter months' drive across the Pennines. Parking was a dream; being a professor gave me a much sought-after parking space in front of my building. I arrived at work feeling excited and positive about the day ahead. I now had a much bigger office, with a secretary looking after my interests: making appointments, taking phone calls and greeting visitors — a tremendous boost to my personal productivity. My office had white walls and a large window at one end, my light-grey desk and blue office chair were near the window and a large meeting table and chairs to match my own stood in the middle of the room. I always had fresh flowers on my desk, with large David Hockney prints in silver frames on my wall and there was a water cooler in the corner. The room felt fresh and calm.

Our Centre of Expertise in e-commerce was in full swing, organising seminars and workshops bringing academics and business together to deepen understanding of the potential opportunities that lay ahead. Some companies were sceptical about the internet because of the so-called 'dot.com bubble'. Early web content providers[68] were grossly overvalued, financial valuations being based on the number of people registered rather than revenue from actual sales. The bubble burst in the spring of 2000 when this false valuation was exposed and some lost as much as 80% of their value on the US stock market [4]. Fortunately, the dot.com bubble hardly affected UK companies, except to make them step cautiously.

One day, my secretary showed in someone who was not at all wary: Kerry Kayes[69], a champion bodybuilder! Kerry said, "I've heard about e-commerce and that the university is keen to help local business. Well, here I am."

"Yes, that's true, er ..."

I was rather taken aback: e-commerce and bodybuilding? Was I slow on the uptake? Had I missed something?

Once seated and offered tea by my secretary, he continued, "I have a sports nutrition business in Denton. We sell into gyms, people ring in their orders or send a fax, we pack them up and post them off. We get a few overseas orders but are

---

[68] Early internet companies Google (started 1998), eBay (started 1995) and Amazon (started 1995)

[69] Kerry Kayes was UK Bodybuilding Fitness Federation (UKBFF) British Champion in 1994

mainly local or UK. We have a great product and want to expand."

I couldn't help looking at him; he had a lovely smile, seemed genuine and refreshing, I was curious.

He told me his company was called CNP Ltd which stood for Chemical Nutrition Products. He could see me look askance. "It's not what you think. All our products are plant-based and manufactured in-house. We are natural bodybuilders and totally discourage the use of steroids."

I felt reassured. Jon had had a spell of bodybuilding while at university and I'd learnt something of it from him. So, odd as it may seem, I felt very positive towards Kerry and his quest for e-commerce. We worked together on a funding bid to the DTI Knowledge Transfer Programme to acquire the staff and resources and to get him up and running.

It was a revelation going to his warehouse to see how his business worked in practice and meeting his staff, nearly all ex-offenders. Kerry took them under his wing, giving them a job in the warehouse on condition that they attended his gym regularly and lead a healthy lifestyle. The programmer/research assistant was rather shocked when he first visited the old warehouse and realised that he would be working there - it was way out of his comfort zone, especially when Kerry said he would expect him to go to the gym too! Kerry kindly created a separate office space for him, the computer equipment was installed and, together with me and one of my e-commerce design team, we developed a detailed design and plan of action.

At first, the challenge was to educate Kerry's right-hand man (and bodybuilder) into better ways of using his existing technology, for example how to use an email list rather than mailing customers individually.

One area of particular interest was Kerry's idea of creating an online community, akin to a 'locker room' in a gym, where people could meet and exchange information about competitions, diets, or exercise routines. Kerry was himself a great asset to the bodybuilding fraternity; everyone wanted to know what he was doing, which competitions he was sponsoring, how his proteges were developing. He was a much-respected man whose advice was valued above all others. Knowledge that Kerry was posting to the online community brought in more readers and, potentially, more customers. The relationship between the online community and e-commerce sales was interesting from a research point of view, and we combined the data gathered on this project with others, to write a paper for the International Journal of e-Commerce [35].

The e-commerce site grew incrementally, giving Kerry and his staff time to reorganise the way they worked and to be trained in how to use the new system. Orders came in from more and more gyms in the UK and across Europe as his site appeared on search engines. Kerry himself was a key advocate, wearing CNP T-shirts in the corner of the boxing ring. He was nutrition adviser to British boxing champion Ricky Hatton at the peak of his career and I remember being irrationally excited when I saw 'cnp.com'– the website we had created – on Kerry's T-shirt during a Sky broadcast of one of Ricky's fights.

His e-commerce business grew like a dream, increasing turnover and profits year on year. By the end of our project, they moved the whole business to a much larger modern warehouse with real offices, and separate toilets for women and men. I was so happy with the work of our university e-commerce design group; my only regret was that we didn't have shares in the business![70]

I loved to help business in this way, to meet such entrepreneurial people with a passion for their business and witness how their business changed. A woman who came to one

[70] The company is now www.cnpprofessional.co.uk

of our early Centre of Expertise in e-Commerce sessions had a small shop selling designer label clothes for children. The shop was located about a mile from the newly opened Trafford Centre[71], and she was worried that customers would go to the mall instead of her local shop. Very quickly, she picked up on the idea of having a website to advertise her business and set about writing her own, asking for help only occasionally. She taught herself HTML and CSS[72] and handcrafted her own site by trial and error. An amazing thing happened; she had lots of hits from America. Aside from designer clothes, she also sold handmade christening dresses that the Americans just loved. She entered into dialogue with each customer and asked them to send photos of the baby wearing the dress, so of course, pictures of beautiful babies brought lots of viewers to the site and lots more customers. All her transactions were by email or online chat, which was enough for her. I was greatly impressed by her determination to grow her business in her own way, using her own talents, ensuring that at every step she was in control and understood the inner workings of her internet business. Her business is still thriving[73]

A key focus for our Centre was the conference[74] in November, bringing together both national and international businesses and universities. The Manchester-based businesses decided to host an e-commerce awards dinner to run alongside the conference. We booked several tables for the Centre and our guests and I took part in judging the awards. I particularly

---

[71] https://en.wikipedia.org/wiki/Trafford_Centre The Trafford Centre is one of the largest indoor shopping malls in the UK located in Greater Manchester

[72] HTML (the Hypertext Markup Language) and CSS (Cascading Style Sheets) are two of the core technologies for building Web pages

[73] Petit Posh https://www.petitposh.co.uk/

[74] Title of conference Innovation through Electronic Commerce, IeC2000, Manchester, UK, 14/11/2000 to 16/11/2000

remember being asked to judge a website that sold perfumes and cosmetics; I was paired with another woman who was very negative about the site. She said, "It doesn't do anything; it just has one page!" What she hadn't worked out was that if you clicked on any word that was underlined you were then taken to another page. It was quite a revelation when I showed her, but after all it was the year 2000 and the internet and e-commerce were still very new to most people.

The conference was great fun; everyone pitched in to make it a success. Jon came in for a couple of weeks in his summer holiday from university to help us raise sponsorship for welcome drinks, advertising, and fees for guest speakers. He telephoned my contacts, explaining about the conference and the benefits for them. I once overheard the phone conversation, amid much laughter, "So Professor Macaulay is your Mum?". It seemed to amuse everyone! He raised over £25,000. I was impressed; Jon was good at sealing a deal and he was calling the right people at BT, ICL, IBM, Royal Mail, Manchester City Council, Co-operative Bank and Manchester Evening News – all active members of our Centre.

We were excited to have attracted Patricia Hewitt[75], Minister of State for Small Business and e-Commerce to open the conference and take part in a panel session alongside our more senior business representatives. It was quite a performance having a minister of state arrive; she had an entourage of security, timekeepers and secretaries keeping an eye on whom she met. She was whisked in, did her duty and then was whisked out to her next appointment. Luckily, I was on her agenda and was able to exchange a few words about the importance of e-commerce to small businesses and what great work was going on in Manchester. On the same day, I'd been invited onto the BBC Breakfast programme to talk about e-

75 https://members.parliament.uk/member/340/career

commerce and its future for business, and of course slipped in a mention of the conference.

Users were flocking to the internet and overseas students were signing up in droves to our new master's degree in e-commerce. These were heady days indeed, with everyone interested in potential new ways of making money. I taught the main module with the title 'e-Commerce', which had a section on privacy and security. Encryption was dealt with in another, more mathematical module, while I covered the business side. In one lecture, when I was talking about the ways in which the security of e-commerce systems could be compromised, for example, by theft of credit card numbers by data breaches or malware, a student asked me, "Why not acquire a list of credit card numbers from another business if you can?"

Taken aback, I looked at her, thinking, 'I'm assuming that everyone has the same ethical stance as me'.

Seemingly sincere, she added, "Surely, if you can make a business from selling credit card numbers, then that is a good thing".

I thought, 'Is this what I am doing, explaining how fraudulent systems work so the students can use them for the wrong reasons?' It was wrong, at least from my point of view.

It was a stark reminder that the internet was still like the 'Wild West', with good guys and bad guys in constant battle, businesses trying to protect their firewalls and baddies attacking them with ever newer and more inventive malware.

Decentralisation of the web means, rightly, that no-one and no organisation has overall control. Unfortunately, it also means that every individual, group, company and government must learn to protect their own privacy and security.

Chapter 13 Privacy and security

Nothing could have prepared us for the 9/11 terrorist attacks in New York. 11th September 2001 was a Tuesday and one of those days when everyone remembers exactly where they were. I was at work when I heard colleagues shouting

"Quick Linda look at this"

"Incredible! - what on earth is happening?"

"Oh no! - it can't be"

They sounded so urgent that I rushed across. Live on the internet - an aeroplane was crashing into one of the 110 storey Twin Towers of the World Trade Centre. As smoke billowed out from the North Tower a second hijacked plane struck the South Tower. They both started to collapse as we watched glued to the screen. It sent shivers up my spine. I'd been to the top of one of the towers with my family only a few years earlier, it could have been us up there.

Everyone was shocked, the unthinkable, the impossible had happened. The world, my world, suddenly seemed very insecure. It was a stark reminder of the level of hostility and hatred some people feel.

This was a physical attack no doubt coordinated via the internet. Though the internet was founded with good intentions the lack of centralised control left it open to abuse. Those who wanted to infiltrate government information systems, steal secrets from business, attack individuals, share knowledge of making bombs or planning attacks had the ideal platform.

Individuals, governments, and business were increasingly storing sensitive data online and consequently making them potential targets of hostile forces whether they be driven by ideology or financial gain. I was concerned about the increasing threat to information security.

Conversations within our e-commerce centre confirmed my fears. One of our collaborators, Martin, was Head of Information Security for the Co-op Bank and for 'smile the internet bank'. Each time we met he had a new story about attacks on their computer firewalls. Typically he would say:

"We had over 10,000 attacks this morning before I left the office, mostly minor but we did manage to harness several trojans[76]."

Martin was a very serious man, always calm but a worrier. He was in his early fifties, hardly ever smiled or laughed. He had plenty to worry about, the hackers[77] were getting cleverer and more organised, and it was a constant race to get one step ahead.

"Do you have any potential hackers among your students?" he asked me one morning.

---

[76] a Trojan is malicious software which misleads users of its true intent. The term is derived from the Ancient Greek story in Virgil's Aeneid of the deceptive Trojan Horse that led to the fall of the city of Troy

[77] Hackers find weaknesses in systems typically to commit fraud, insert hostile code (malware) or steal a person's identity.

"Hackers?" I said naively thinking he would want to avoid them.

"Yes, we employ them to see if they can find weaknesses in our system - if they can get through the firewall. We need 'good' hackers - friendly, with strong ethical values who want to use their talents for good. We pay them well."

"Ah" I replied "you want to see if they can discover flaws in your firewall's code before the hostile hackers do - maybe I could introduce you to one potential student". Though I wasn't at all sure that I knew students well enough to assess their ethical stance.

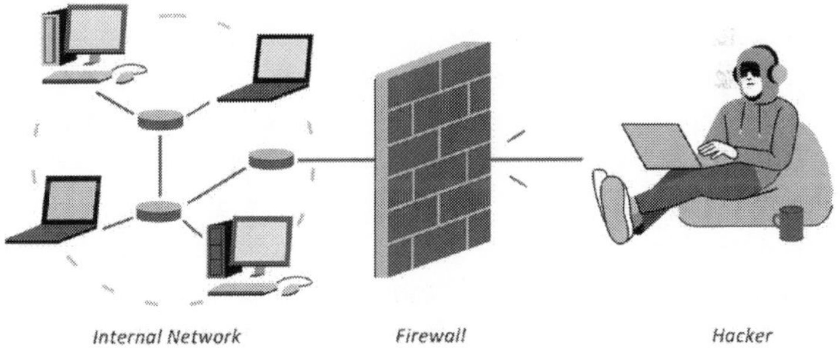

I felt concerned, every day was a constant battle for Martin as he sought to protect the bank from attacks and I wondered how he coped with the constant negativity.

His boss on the other hand was a lively fellow. He could see the bigger picture and as Director of Technology at the Co-op bank had to deal with a wide range of people - traditionalists and modernisers, business and technical.

Keith could foresee problems for internet banking: technological problems caused by external attacks; internal problems caused by the insecure behaviour of staff; safety problems for the bank caused by customer ignorance of how to protect themselves online.

I liked Keith a great deal; he was a family man in his fifties, a tall solid figure with strong black hair who spent his weekends playing golf. He had a strong ethical stance and truly believed in the Co-op's own policy of fairness and social inclusion[78]. He had a sense of personal responsibility to society as well as to the bank. Highly competent of course, his was a strategic, technical, leadership position.

Keith would tell us tales of when he first got promoted to Director and was given access to the private car park at the Co-op HQ in Central Manchester. He would arrive in his car, a concierge would take his keys, park the car for him and once a week valet the car - old fashioned luxury alas no longer! He liked to feel important, puff up his feathers and smile.

We got on well; now that I was a professor and head of the e-commerce centre, he treated me as an equal and seemed proud to show me off to his colleagues. Naturally this made me smile and puff up my own feathers just a little. He took me to the executive dining room at the bank where I could meet the board members. To my surprise prayers were said before dinner, not rushed at all, everyone stood heads bowed and seemed really sincere. It was a different world, harking back to its founding fathers in the nineteenth century[79] and I felt that Keith wanted me to see the world that the Co-operative Bank was emerging from. The technological revolution was at their door, and some were reluctant to enter.

---

[78] The Co-operative Bank is the only UK high street bank with a customer-led Ethical Policy which is incorporated into the Bank's Articles of Association

[79] The bank was formed in 1872 as the Loan and Deposit Department of the Co-operative Wholesale Society, becoming the CWS Bank four years later. However, the bank did not become a registered company until 1971.

Technology was his passion; he had embraced the internet and proudly showed me the bank's laboratory equipped with all the latest devices. Every type of phone, tablet, laptop ready for testing the next version of the internet bank. Internet fraud was on the rise and Keith was responsible for keeping it under control. All banks absorbed an amount of fraud but if it got above a certain threshold the bank would be subject to investigation by the Financial Services Authority and Keith definitely wanted to avoid that.

He was a holistic thinker, could see both internal threats and external threats, both intentional and unintentional.

Keith explained about potential internal risks: "I'm concerned about security within the bank, not that I think the staff are acting fraudulently but we did prosecute one case and it made me think how easy it is to get into our systems if you know the passwords."

"We can investigate – find out what is happening now and see what can be done. The solution may be technological or behavioural". I replied:

"Look at passwords first, staff typically have access to three different internal systems and every month they are issued with a new randomly generated password for each one."

Through the centre for e-commerce we had attracted funding from the Economic and Social Science Research Council and the UK Government Department of Trade and Industry to investigate and propose solutions to a number of privacy and security problems. We focussed mainly on human interaction with technology where we acted as neutral investigators, to find out but not to assign blame. The project was called 'Human Issues in Privacy and Security in e-Commerce' - HiSPEC for short.

We were fortunate to have psychologist Dr Kathy Keeling on our team. She was a warm, friendly person who bank staff would readily trust in conversation. A talented research scientist with a logical, analytical mind. One of the key problems Kathy found was that staff couldn't remember the secure passwords given them by the technical staff and immediately replaced them with their own.

Kathy had asked staff, "How do you choose a password?" They replied:

"The name of my pet"

"My children's names"

"We have family passwords - if one of us thinks of a good password we all use it"

"I use the same password for everything but with a suffix of the name of the system I'm using"

"I alternate passwords each month"

Kathy asked, "How do you remember a password?"

"Put a sticker on my desk"

"Write it on a pad in my drawer"

"Keep a photo on my desk as a reminder"

"Put them on my pinboard at home next to the shopping list"

I must admit to having adopted a number of these myself knowing it was risky, but you really do have to be self-disciplined to change. In any case, I rationalised, I don't work for a bank.

It was easy for a staff member to guess the password of another. The office cleaners had free access in the evenings and if motivated to do so could collect enough scraps of information to deduce passwords.

The question in my mind was "even if others could find out staff passwords what would they do with them?"

Keith: "You only need one malicious person to steal passwords and sell them on the internet. Once through the firewall hackers could have a field day getting into customer accounts and transferring money between accounts."

We trialled a number of technological solutions, such as storing passwords on smart cards. In parallel we mounted a social marketing campaign to change staff behaviour - to persuade them to keep their desks clear of password clues, to use passphrases to devise a memorable password, to log out/shut down when leaving, to introduce checks on password strength. Kathy led on the design of the campaign which of course would only work if staff were willing, and Keith gave them direction.

I decided to change my attitude towards passwords too.

Unlike the intentional hostility of external hackers, the insecure behaviour of internal staff was unintentional.

Was it safe to use the internet, was my own data safe online? Use of the internet had many advantages but tech people in business were not upskilling fast enough. We were seeing a growth in programmers without professional qualifications setting up websites; some of my first-year students were already running the family's business site.

My question was - once I entered data into a website what happened to it?

The 1998 Data Protection Act sought to answer that question by providing legally binding guidance on what personal data can be collected and how it should be stored and processed.

If e-commerce was to grow, then people needed to trust that their information is protected and that it remains under their control. In my view this could only happen if databases and software were designed with data protection in mind from the outset.

There were eight principles in essence saying that data should only be held for the purpose for which it was intended; that the data be accurate and adequate; that it should only be retained for the agreed period; that it be fair, lawful, and secure;

and that it may only be transferred to countries who upheld similar data protection laws.

So, what was really happening in the UK, were organisations complying with the Data Protection Act? As part of our project we put a team together to find out[80]. We compared what companies said they would do as stated on their Privacy Statement with what they actually did. We spoke to data controllers and developers within organisations quizzing them about database design and other relevant technical details[81].

Most big businesses, especially those subject to regulation, performed well. However, we found smaller organisations who simply 'cut and paste' a Privacy Statement from someone else's website and put it on theirs - failing to make any actual link with the way data was held or processed. The general understanding of data protection was poor; when quizzed on data security one small company told us "…oh yes our data is very secure. We store it on floppy discs[82] and at the end of the day lock them in a drawer."

They hadn't quite grasped that it wasn't so much where the data is physically stored but what happens to it when their system is live and on the internet.

Of the eight principles, the one most often flaunted was that of retention. For example, websites would ask users if they wanted their credit details stored, the user would say NO but the company would store them anyway. Other examples include the 'tick box'; a user ticks a box to say they don't want

---

[80] we had direct contact with 900 companies and organisations and visited 3000 urls – part of the HiSPEC project

[81] http://www.lindamacaulay.co.uk/upload/resource/9_1dpacompliancereport.pdf

[82] Floppy discs were on their way out but still used with older PCs. (Apple still shipping 3 ¼" floppies upto 1998)

any further information from a company, but the company sends it anyway.

Following this study the Office of the Information Commissioner[83] had asked me to work with them. They wanted me to develop guidelines for software designers to explain when and where the key principles of the Act should be incorporated into the design. The Act itself was a large legal document rather than something that software engineers would read so the idea was to distil the main points into a guidance document setting out what they should do at each stage of the process[84].

Would the internet ever be a safe place? The bank was no different to other organisations, they all faced the same problems. Privacy and security are intimately related. Individuals and businesses have the right to control their own information (privacy) and the right to protect or know how their information is protected (security).

The 9/11 attacks were unthinkable but did actually happen. I felt that the level of threat to the online world was increasing, and we were yet to experience the 'unthinkable'. The unintentional lapses in security by a company's staff and the careless attitudes towards an individual's privacy add to the insecurity of the internet as much as the intentional, external hostile attacks of hackers.

While continuing to work on the project I was also keen to contribute to the department as a whole, everyone seemed really stressed and I felt I should at least try to improve the situation.

---

[83] https://ico.org.uk

[84] http://www.lindamacaulay.co.uk/upload/resource/farstarsbpdmay02.pdf

Chapter 14 Leadership

Statue of Emmeline Pankhurst, St. Peter's Square, Manchester

My life had been spent in one male-dominated workplace after another; it was 2002 and I'd had no direct experience of a female leader. Where should I look for a suitable role model? Which women did I admire? You might say that Margaret Thatcher, the first female Prime Minister, was an obvious choice. I quite liked the way she dressed, with her business-style suits, the fact that she wore a skirt and didn't adopt the male attire of trousers and I was amused that she managed to turn a noun into a verb (handbag into handbagging)[85]. But I found nothing inspiring in her leadership style.

The two women I admired most were Barbara Castle [36], a fearless, exceptional politician who, in 1970, introduced the Equal Pay Act, and Emmeline Pankhurst [37], a political activist who fought for women's suffrage. Both were born in northern

[85] Handbag as a verb, Macmillan dictionary: if a woman handbags someone, she argues with them forcefully and gets them to do what she wants. *I met Mrs Thatcher at the ambassador's residence and she handbagged me*

England, fought tirelessly for the causes they believed in, succeeded against all odds to change prevailing attitudes and didn't let the fact that they were women stand in their way. They had self-belief.

Barbara Castle questioned why women had more belief in men than themselves: "I marvel at women's instinctive acceptance of men's belief in their own superiority." Giving out prizes at a girls school, "Shyness," she told them, "is a form of vanity. It means you are thinking more about yourself than about your subject or your audience. Put them first and your shyness will disappear." Further, about all girls, "the most important skill they could acquire was self-confidence." [36] p37

"Think of your subject and your audience", "Be self-confident", "Have self-belief." These were messages I took forward when becoming head of Department of Computation, the first female head since its founding in 1968.

I decided that the department was my subject and not to let the fact that I was a woman stand in my way.

But what leadership style should I adopt? How had others led?

When I first joined the department, the head was a 'command-and-control' type, autocratic, with a tendency to give orders, and you were expected to do as he asked. He had been head for a while, and when he retired, the department adopted a more modern approach: it was to be run by a committee of professors, with each professor taking turn to be head for a period of two or three years.

Among those who followed, there were varying levels of actual involvement in departmental affairs. One was rather laissez-faire, enjoying the status but not wanting any of the problems, being more interested in his own research and business. The next was more authoritative, with a vision of how things should be done, fully engaging with the department, introducing new ways of working and creating lots of opportunities for growth. The one immediately before me was initially consultative and democratic but as time went on became more autocratic. He was keen to please the Vice-Chancellor, saying yes to his requests a little too often with one eye on his next promotion.

How should I go forward? I had led and built up teams in the past based on a shared vision and direction, had successfully acted as facilitator of small decision-making groups and had an understanding of difficult people and how to deal with them. Was I autocratic? No. I didn't want to tell people what to do; I wanted to win over hearts and minds so that they would want to come on the journey with me - but would I be perceived as weak?

"Masculine stereotypes of leadership can leave women caught between either adopting that persona or appearing as weak" [38] p171 – a subject of some debate. Abbate [38] quotes from her interview with Fran Bergman[86], the first female director of San Diego Supercomputer Center, appointed in 2001: " …if people know you are a reasonably nice person, a team player, they don't think you are going to make hard decisions; they don't think you're necessarily credible…..Because you're not what people expect a director to look like."

Bergman also suggested that women needed models of toughness that they could relate to: "One thing that I think is really true is that what drives me is not necessarily what drives my (male) colleagues … Sometimes I think my colleagues go out there and their mental image is 'Kill the infidels!' …And I always go out there and I think, 'I must protect my cubs!'" [38]p172

"Protect my cubs"; I'm not sure that ever occurred to me, though I did feel more like nurturing the staff than attacking them.

[86] Fran Bergman, Computer Scientist, https://en.wikipedia.org/wiki/Francine_Berman accessed 18/05/20.

I felt a facilitative leadership style would suit me best, allowing staff to contribute, empowering them to grow and develop as individuals, giving them a sense of ownership and direction within their own groups and energising them into a shared vision for the whole department. I didn't feel that this was weak leadership, though it might be perceived as such by those used to an autocratic or authoritarian style. This was my style and I was determined to make it work.

I saw three main challenges: grossly overworked staff; an undercurrent of sexual harassment; feuding factions within staff groups – and overriding all these was the need for a renewed sense of purpose and direction.

The first challenge: overworked staff

This wasn't going to be easy. One of my first tasks was to allocate teaching and admin duties[87] to the thirty-five academics. There were two sides to this; first, that all the departmental duties must be covered to ensure its smooth running and, second, that each academic had a fair workload and one that satisfied their individual needs in terms of knowledge, skills and aspirations.

A daunting and exhausting first task: some academics were lovely, they were happy with the allocation and accepted the extra duties demanded by our circumstances; others were incredibly awkward, refusing to do a fair workload, but instead insisting that it wasn't their fault that the department had too much work; one or two maintained we were teaching the wrong

---

[87] At UMIST an academic's time should be spent: one-third teaching, one-third research and one-third admin related to either teaching or admin. If they had too much teaching, then their research would suffer. Academics were continuously trying to cope with two very different sets of demands: excellence in research and excellence in teaching. Promotion was more directly linked to research than teaching.

subjects and asked why their proposal for a new module hadn't been accepted; some just wanted to argue about everything.

It was a good introduction to what was to come. I had a better understanding of who the 'difficult' people would be but also sensed more irritability, impatience and aggressiveness than usual. Staff were under a lot of pressure; some found the workload overwhelming, while others seemed uninterested as if resigned to the situation. They were visibly stressed.

If I were to achieve that new sense of purpose that we so desperately needed, I had to find a way to reduce staff workload.

The department was a victim of its own success; in addition to the popular B.Sc. Computation, new, highly successful degree titles had been introduced a few years earlier, together with, of course, the new master's in e-Commerce. Student numbers had risen significantly but staff numbers hadn't, and academics were buckling under the strain.

Alongside other computing departments in the UK, ours was a 'cash cow'[88] for the university. Income from all departments went to the university's central coffers and was then redistributed to each department according to its costs. This had the effect that more successful departments like ours subsidised those, physics for example, that were less successful.

Despite a £7million budget, Computation was under-resourced, with staff-student ratios much higher than in other Russell group[89] universities with staff supervising unmanageable numbers of master's and Doctoral students. Something had to be done.

---

[88] A 'cash cow' is a venture that generates a steady return of profits that far exceeds the outlay of cash required to run it.

[89] The Russell Group represents 24 leading UK universities https://russellgroup.ac.uk.

Fortunately, I had Rosemary, a constant and a most capable professional administrator, a kind of 'Head of Civil Service' who understood our finances. We worked together for months trying to put together a business plan to take to the Vice-Chancellor to ask for more resources. You would expect the plan to say, 'Give us this amount of money and you will get these benefits in return,' but the university already had the benefits. Instead, we were asking for more money to do the same job that we were already doing.

We hit on the idea of producing a 'negative' business plan. It would set out, in financial terms, what would happen if we didn't get the investment: dissatisfied students; loss of reputation; reduction in student numbers; absenteeism and loss of staff through stress; inability of staff to do research and consequent loss of research income.

We worked out that we needed another 15 staff in addition to our current 35. That was a lot!

You can imagine that this wasn't going to be a popular plan, not least with the other heads of department, because every £1 the university gave us was £1 less in their pockets! I worked hard to lobby the other heads, to explain our case in person and to think of everything I could to win over hearts and minds and articulate the longer-term benefits for them.

Eventually, the Vice-Chancellor agreed that I could make our case to the Academic Board and he would take advice from them. The meeting was in the boardroom, involving the VC, the registrar and twelve or so heads of department[90]. I had a feeling of déjà vu, as if it were my interview all over again, just me and a room full of men. The Board members had their papers in front of them; looking around I could see those I had lobbied in person and others that I hadn't. Oh dear, I should have done more.

[90] UMIST didn't have faculties; departments reported directly to the Vice-Chancellor.

Trying to be calm and logical, I presented the argument and outlined the investment needed. I got through it somehow, answering their questions, being well-versed in both numbers and arguments. I had the vision and the detail.

It was impossible to stay detached and business-like when staff were under so much stress and willing me to succeed. I became emotional: there was no other woman in the room. Were they going to think I was menopausal? My voice almost broke, tears welling in my eyes. Take a deep breath, calm down! I felt so passionate about the case; I just couldn't help showing it.

We waited over a week for the decision, relayed at first by phone, then in writing. We were delighted to be given extra resources over the next three years, not the 15 we'd asked for, but 13.5 full-time staff. Amazing. We could start recruiting. There was light at the end of the tunnel for the overworked academics and a general sigh of relief all round. I was told that my display of passion had moved the Board: "They had never seen a head close to tears in the cause of their department."

Perhaps I was 'protecting my cubs' after all!

The challenges I'd set myself were in addition to my job of teaching, research and the day-to-day running of the department. We had to keep a tight ship; together with Cath my secretary we managed my diary in 20-minute slots, no group meeting would last more than an hour and we had a rolling plan for each day, week, three weeks and three months. Jon would have been impressed, he frequently quoted from Benjamin Franklin[91]: "If you fail to plan, you are planning to fail!"

Given the size of the job, Patrick suggested that I stay over in Manchester a few nights a week instead of driving to and from work each day. We bought a small apartment near the university in a block with a pool and gym; it was lovely to go for

[91] Benjamin Franklin, 1706 -1790, an American polymath and one of the founding fathers of the United States.

an early-morning swim. Patrick loved it too and it wasn't long before we were spending the weekends enjoying the cinemas, theatres and city living. By this time the children had all just about moved out from the family home in Halifax and we were beginning to think it was time that we moved out too.

The second challenge: undercurrent of sexual harassment.

The imbalance between male and female academics was still stark and I very much hoped we would see some well-qualified women applying for the new posts.

When I first started in the department it felt quite aggressive, with only one other female academic. By the time I took over as head, we had recruited two further female academics, bringing our number to four, and we also had a female industrial liaison officer. What would the atmosphere be like for female applicants? Would it still feel aggressive? I wasn't sure. Nevertheless, I still felt there was an undercurrent of unspoken, unconscious sexism that needed to be brought to the surface and dealt with. I had heard snippets of conversation: "Oh, he always asks me to assign him the female dissertation students."

"Sometimes, you know, he goes to their house."

"He has a reputation for the girls; he likes it if they have IT problems."

– rumblings that made me uncomfortable.

Was it just gossip or was there something more going on?

We ran a conversion course that was relatively popular with women, where the students had a first degree in another subject and wanted to convert into Computing. One year our master's students protested against the use of sexist language in our lectures.

"Why are Systems Analysts always referred to as 'he'? Are all programmers male? You never use the words 'she' or 'her'; it makes us feel as though you are not talking about us; we feel excluded."

The academic staff, including me, were taken aback, never having even thought about the language we used. They presented us with a feminist analysis of our lecture materials and the embedded sexism was stark. We all had to change. We had to recognise the importance of language if we were to create a fairer study and working environment for women.

I wanted to have a better understanding of what was going on more broadly, and called all the female staff to a meeting in my office. I didn't email, but instead took the time to speak to each one with a personal invitation; it was to be over a sandwich lunch, so there was no need to ask the permission of their professor to come. I knew it would take time to get them to trust each other enough to speak out, so I planned for a monthly get-together and persuaded everyone to promise that what was said wouldn't go beyond the meeting room. The men were suspicious of what we were doing, one even listening at the door then pretending to come in by mistake.

It was a delicate and difficult topic, trying to draw out behaviours that had been tolerated for years, that were said to be 'okay', 'no harm meant' or 'just playful banter'. One of the women wouldn't stand any nonsense, telling us that one of the professors would look into her office and, seeing she was alone, come in, walk around her and take photographs. In no uncertain terms she told him to 'f.. off' and got up to show him the door. Another much meeker, younger academic staff member said the professor would come into her office if she was working late and ask about her husband, "Is he away at a conference?" Being polite, and he her superior, she answered "yes". He then moved up close to her, asking what it was like when her husband was away, asking, "Do you feel lonely in bed at night? What do you do to comfort yourself?" This behaviour had been going on for some time; she'd become afraid to stay in her own office, felt intimidated, violated and yet had told no-one about it.

I needed to hear what was going on, so that it could be stopped. A big part of that was to get the meeker, gentler women to toughen up, not to tolerate inappropriate behaviour and to give them the words to use and the attitudes to adopt to repel the offender. The other part was to work out a mechanism for reporting the offence so the offender could be dealt with.

How could we expect to recruit and retain female academics with this sort of behaviour going on?

The university was in the throes of introducing its own procedures for sexual harassment[92] as required by the 2002/73/EC European Directive on the equal treatment of men and women at work, but there was nothing yet at the departmental level.

It was difficult enough to get women to recognise that they were victims of sexual harassment and that they were internalising their embarrassment and shame of the situation. If they were brave enough to speak out, then who would they go to and what would be the consequences for them? Mostly, their bosses were men; any offence had to be put in writing and could only be put forward to the university with the support of the head of department (usually a man and colleague of the offender). It was difficult to see how anything would ever be reported formally.

---

[92]Sexual harassment: where any form of unwanted verbal, non-verbal or physical conduct of a sexual nature occurs, with the purpose or effect of violating the dignity of a person, in particular when creating an intimidating, hostile, degrading, humiliating or offensive environment. European Directive 2002/73/EC .https://eur-lex.europa.eu/LexUriServ/LexUriServ.do?uri=CELEX:32002L0073:EN:HTML accessed 21/05/2020

The most annoying part of the whole thing was the way it undermined women's confidence in themselves. As Barbara Castle rightly said, "the most important skill they could acquire was self-confidence".

It was even more difficult to persuade men to recognise that they were offenders, and to understand what exactly constituted sexual harassment, when they consistently underestimated the level of harassment taking place. It is widely accepted that formal procedures alone are not able to address embedded attitudes. Nonetheless we had to start somewhere. I sent out a memo to all staff giving the definition of sexual harassment, explaining that the department was working with the university to develop procedures for dealing with offenders and asking if anyone would like to join a working party. At least it let the offenders know that something was afoot.

I continued to support the female staff to help them build self-confidence, to give them the tools to repel attempts at harassment and to work with the administration to get departmental procedures in place. Sadly, in my period of office, no formal complaints were forthcoming, but it did seem to affect some of the offenders to know that there might be consequences for their actions. Either that or I was being naïve and the behaviour had just gone further underground.

The third challenge: feuding factions.

We had some wonderful administrators, about 15 in number and all female, some focussed on teaching-related work, others supported the professors and their research teams. I was surprised to discover how many thought of themselves as career women; I don't know why I was surprised – it just hadn't occurred to me. The university was a much sought-after place to work and provided training, annual reviews and a graded profession with opportunity for personal development. Once head of department, I found out more about them; for example, about half didn't have children but they had embarked on a career as professional administrators and that was their main focus.

As a result not many admin staff left and were very much wedded to the role they had carried out for a number of years. However, there was some tension between them; it didn't help that they were on five different floors within the tower block. I decided to practice my facilitation skills and bring them together for a Future Workshop [39] [40] providing me with an opportunity to listen, get to know them better and to try to get to the bottom of it.

These workshops lasted one hour, essentially a structured brainstorming exercise with someone (me in this case) out at the front writing on a flip chart.

Stage 1: Talk about Now - 20 mins: I took my pen in hand and said "Regarding your job or the admin group, what are all the things that are wrong at the moment? Have a good moan, shout out, no discussion, no objections, just shout out and I will write it down."

Stage 2: next what is your Fantasy - 20 mins: I told them to forget about all the problems and fantasise on the future. I said "How would you like things to be, what is your ideal, a year/two years from now, what is your vision, your fantasy? Ideally, don't think about resources or practicalities, fantasise, just shout out and I will write it down."

I put the two sets of flip charts on the wall.

Stage 3: Implementation: 20 mins: We looked at the two charts together quickly reviewed all the problems comparing them with their fantasies and I said: "Given what is wrong now and your ideal/fantasy, identify one or two actions you could take to improve the situation."

Throughout the session I kept hearing the word 'kettle', 'lost kettle', 'my kettle', accusations about a kettle.

"Where was the kettle?"

"I'm sure I saw it in her cupboard."

"She broke it and didn't replace it."

"I'm not speaking to her until I get my kettle back."

It turned out that years ago one admin had borrowed the kettle of another, taken it to their floor and never returned it. They argued over it and went on to involve others.

Once we had got this out in the open, we all started to laugh. "It all boiled down to the kettle!"

It was time to get over it. It was long ago and by now they all had perfectly good working kettles!

Despite the kettle argument they came up with some great ideas.

One idea was that the department should have its own café where they could socialise and get on better as a group. They agreed to help me follow up, lobby for wider staff support, help find the right person to run it, while I looked for funds. We were all quite excited.

Another issue they identified was IT; admin was always moaning about tech support. I agreed to facilitate a discussion between the two groups. I asked them to send me a list of issues beforehand.

There were around 10 IT staff who supported all staff, student labs, network servers and computers and provided some specialist programming for research groups.

The IT support staff, mostly men, were much less communicative. I tried the Future Workshop with them, but many simply were not used to expressing their views in an open forum. They were also distrustful of my motives. "Why is she asking us our opinion?", "We just fix office computers and run student laboratories." Fortunately, there were exceptions: those IT staff who supported academic research projects were more innovative and open. It was invaluable for me to learn about this group of staff early in my leadership so I could investigate alternative strategies to engage them.

Naturally, everyone assumed that IT staff were there just for them and couldn't understand why they had to wait. When IT and admin staff eventually got together they softened their attitudes towards each other. The IT staff decided to bring forward a plan for job scheduling and recording so that admin staff (and others) would know when their problem would be fixed if they couldn't fix it straight away.

I wanted to create an atmosphere of mutual respect and understanding so they could all work better together, not only within their own group but also alongside other groups.

The overriding challenge: a renewed sense of purpose.

The academics were of course by far the largest group in the department, and together we needed to renew our sense of purpose and direction. Computation was originally a sub-department of Mathematics, and from the outset had had an emphasis on application and use of computing rather than the technology-focused approaches of many mainstream computer science departments[93]. We had grown and diversified over the years and needed to reassess and reaffirm our mission.

I knew that getting academics on board with my vision for change would be a long game, requiring a series of group meetings and staff away days to ensure their involvement in decision-making and buy-in for my ultimate goal: a new name and change of direction for the department.

After consulting with the committee of professors, I organised a series of staff 'awaydays'; we didn't go anywhere except just to a nice room on campus but outside the department. I ran a series of facilitated workshops.

Some academics behaved like prima donnas, with an inflated view of their own talent or importance and expecting to be treated as special; not at all the kind who likes to 'join in'.

[93] JISC Archives Hub: UMIST Department of Computation Archive. https://archiveshub.jisc.ac.uk/search/archives/5c1460fa-4689-38e8-af05-9039f97271a9 accessed 25/05/20

Others were more agreeable, open to new ideas and willing to take part. Some had the kind of introverted personality often associated with computer programmers or engineers. It was going to be a challenge to rally this diverse group and reach any kind of consensus.

Initially, staff gave presentations of their work to ensure everyone knew what their colleagues were doing. You may (or may not) be surprised that academic staff often don't know what their colleagues in the next room are doing.

Next we suggested a number of research themes, and asked staff to sit at the table of the one they felt more comfortable with, so they could identify areas for future collaboration and reassess the themes. We documented the emerging themes and came to the next workshop with a proposal of the key research areas and how they fitted together.

Finally, we agreed on a simplified model that could be used to describe our research. Most agreed that we were still mainly concerned with the application and use of computers. The model was represented by a Venn diagram with three overlapping circles: data and information, people and organisations, software and technology. Most research lay within the intersections; for example, Information Systems lay between 'people and organisations' and 'data and information', Artificial Intelligence lay between 'data and information' and 'software and technology', Human Computer Interaction lay at the intersection of all three, and so on. With only one exception (there is always one!) everyone could see where their research would fit.

Over a number of years, the department had become more interdisciplinary, introducing teaching driven by real business problems that required students to think in a holistic way, to work in teams and to draw on a range of taught modules. We had an active industrial advisory panel that wanted graduates with high levels of interpersonal skills as well as technical skills, and we had made efforts to design the curriculum accordingly.

We felt that we had a special offering with a focus significantly different from traditional Computer Science, and wanted to stay together with a renewed sense of purpose and direction.

To reflect this renewed focus of collective research, we decided to change our name from the Department of Computation to the School of Informatics, taking into account the names of other top university research departments moving in a similar direction to us.

I didn't achieve all this on my own; the department was run by the committee of professors and we had our own awaydays to sort out ideas between us. We did actually go away somewhere nice! Most of the professors supported the academic staff workshops and, though not necessarily agreeing with everything, helped to move things forward.

I've described all this as a logical process but, in fact, it was a highly emotional journey for me and for many of the academics. There were rumblings of a merger between UMIST and the Victoria University of Manchester and we needed to clarify who we were and where we would fit in any new structure.

My time as head of department was over too soon; I had enjoyed it and wanted to continue. I had been just over two years in post, from 2001 to 2003. The university decided that a new person was needed to carry forward our renewed vision into the merger discussion. I was invited to sit on the Project Unity board, a high-powered group with representatives from both universities with responsibility for guiding pre-merger decisions.

Had I adopted the right leadership style?

I got as far as I could with the three challenges, and the 'early win' of getting more resources really helped because it gave the impression that I 'could get things done'.

The admin staff did get their café. We worked hard to secure the resources to set it up and recruited a lovely, kind woman to run it, greeting us with a smile, providing us with lunches and coffees and generally creating a home-from-home atmosphere. I really loved it and it helped continue the dialogue between staff.

I continued my quest to get women to speak to me in confidence if they experienced any form of harassment, though even with reporting procedures in place I knew that most women would be reluctant to report a male colleague. Much more work was needed to change attitudes.

The facilitative style worked well. I felt comfortable, and once staff got used to it, I felt they respected my integrity and developed a sense of trust and co-operation.

Now it was time to get back in to research; my group and colleagues had been wonderfully supportive of my role. No longer head of department, I needed to re-assess my place in the world.

Chapter 15 The invisible wife

It's not easy being a woman. Living in a man's world is a constant, yet expectations of women keep changing. What does society want of us? When men went off to fight in the world wars, women worked in munition factories or on the farms, doing the man's work while he was away. When he returned the woman was told to go back in the kitchen, it being her moral duty to devote herself to the family. Between the WWII and the swinging sixties she was expected to be seductively feminine and focus on how she looked. There were periods during which she was considered a bad wife and mother for wanting to go out to work and earn her own living and other periods when she was an even worse wife and mother for not being eager to do so [41]. Women have tried, and are still trying, to liberate themselves from the control of male power structures and, despite attempts to remove gender discrimination, the underlying behaviours linger on. It's no wonder women feel confused.

If I ever needed to be reminded of my 'place' in the world, I just had to go to my husband's workplace near Bradford. It was a long-established family business, founded in 1840 and successfully handed down through the generations. They owned a large housing stock for rental and built new homes for sale. Patrick was the yard foreman; managing the building supplies, making sure all the site workers had what they needed and generally kept everything moving. He is an honest and industrious man with a great sense of humour and was very much liked by both bosses and workers.

It was a place where there were the 'bosses'; the family members were all directors and each had a share in the business. It was the family's birthright to be directors and their sons went to the best private schools. Every Christmas they organised a very generous party for the thirty or so workers and their wives, who mostly lived in Queensbury, a small working-class town nearby. They usually booked the golf club where the bosses were members. It was quite an occasion. Everyone turned out in their best suit and tie or new dress. There was one free drink on arrival, a traditional Christmas dinner, bottles of wine on the table, a raffle then a disco.

The bosses were friendly but, at the same time, kept aloof from the workers. When Patrick arrived, he was called over: they thought him quite a character, remarked on what he was wearing, laughed and joked together. They'd say hello to me:

"This is my wife, Linda."

"I'm so pleased to meet you." His boss bowed slightly.

"Good to meet you, too." I held my hand out to shake his as I would if I were at work; with the lightest of touch his hand made contact with mine, giving me the impression he'd rather not bother.

"Now Patrick, what were we saying?"

.... I became invisible.

As the wife of one of the workers, I was not important in my own right, but merely an addendum, not included in the conversation. I noticed it was the same for the other wives. I found this behaviour puzzling and archaic. I tried to join in but found my attempts at conversation were not reciprocated.

At first, I felt somewhat deflated by their attitude, but then it amused me; I thought I'd returned to the Victorian era when the working classes and the women were kept in their place.

I'd heard of 'the Invisible Wife Syndrome', a term used by Edna Healey, wife of Denis who was Chancellor of the Exchequer under Harold Wilson's government in the 1970s. She commented that, despite her having met Wilson on numerous occasions, he only ever spoke to her twice. She too felt invisible, so in fact she took it upon herself to make other 'invisible wives' visible by writing a book about them called 'Wives of Fame' [42].

My husband wasn't even famous, yet in this man's world I was still made to feel invisible. I thought I'd achieved a great deal. Indeed, yes, I had achieved a great deal – first female professor, leader, computer scientist – I was sure of that. But none of it mattered here because I was the wife and should know my place. I wasn't so much confused as bemused.

Did Patrick and I just inhabit different worlds? He came to the professorial dinner parties with me, and I went to the works dinners with him, but that's just how it was: a divided existence full of contradictions.

I suppose it was odd for Patrick too, though I hope in a nice way, because shortly after the works Christmas dinner I was to attend a conference in Hawaii, and he didn't hesitate to come with me.

I could forget about being the wife and the departmental leader for a while; I could enjoy being myself, presenting and discussing research with fellow enthusiasts at the January 2004 Hawaii International Conference on System Science. It was the place to be seen and meet researchers I very much admired. The proceedings were published worldwide by IEEE[94]. It would re-energise my research.

We had decided to combine my attendance at the conference with a much-needed holiday and to be away for three weeks. We had a family Christmas at home and then, feeling slightly guilty for not taking our teenage daughters with us, set off on December 28th, 2003.

Our first stop was Los Angeles; we were excited to see the city for the first time. We spent most of our time in Hollywood, seeing the Walk of Fame and the Hollywood sign. We celebrated New Year in a lounge bar on Sunset Boulevard and explored the city using public transport. Such great contrasts: the extremely rich Beverly Hills and the very poor San Pedro.

[94] IEEE (Institute of Electrical and Electronic Engineering). https://www.ieee.org

It was raining when we left L.A. and, after we had travelled 3,300 miles west to Hawaii, it was still raining! I had no idea it was so far, entailing a six-hour flight. The conference venue, the Hilton Hotel, was large and rather pretentious, with tropical birds, fish and palm trees. The complex consisted of three large hotels connected by waterways, and guests got around on boats or a small train. Our room, overlooking the Pacific Ocean, was idyllic, though you can imagine how expensive everything was.

My paper was in the Human Computer Interaction stream and was reporting on experimental research we had done on embodied conversational agents, contributing to the debate in online retailing questioning whether avatars could replace people from a call centre and, if so, what would they look like [43]. At the conference I also attended sessions on systems thinking, for I was becoming more interested in how everything is connected and wanted to learn about the interdisciplinary field of systems science.

Once the conference was over, we took a short flight to Honolulu. We stayed at the Pacific Monarch on the 22nd floor in an amazing apartment with a view of the beach and a roof-top pool. The apartment doors opened out, concertina style, leaving the rooms totally accessible to the balcony; it was like being outside but 22 floors up – a bit scary, at first.

Our most moving experience was the visit to the USS Arizona Memorial at Pearl Harbor, the site of the 1941 Second World War Japanese attack on American ships while anchored in harbour. The bodies of over a thousand sailors and marines still lie in the sea directly below the floating memorial, so you couldn't help but be affected by the experience.

We had a wonderful time together, but the journey home was incredibly long, over 24 hours. We were glad to return home for a rest.

My husband's bosses may not have been very aware of it, but technology was moving apace. A new slow boom in e-commerce was taking place, and real value was being gained from internet businesses with Google's initial public offering on the stock market in 2004. Social media was coming onstream, first Myspace in 2003 then Facebook in 2004, and there was increasing interest in the commercialisation of avatars and virtual worlds. So much more to discover.

I felt re-energised and ready for work.

Chapter 16 The digital divide

It was lovely having my own research group just along the corridor from my office. They occupied a large open-plan laboratory with individual work areas comprising a desk, computer, filing cabinet and a cupboard for their personal bits and pieces. In the centre of the room were easy chairs where we could sit and chat and create a sense of belonging. An industrious group of about 8 or 9 at any one time, some working on funded projects, others being doctoral students funded by their government or university.

Having my group around me was like wearing a cosy, oversize sweater. We were comfortable together and trusted each other, even though we were from very different backgrounds.

Mauricette, for example, was originally a solicitor who having seen IT systems in use at work thought she could probably do better and decided to study for our master's in Computation to convert into computing. A truly remarkable woman from Switzerland, always smartly dressed, had a logical mind and an attention to detail. Mauricette became the project manager for our Centre of Expertise in e-Commerce and all our business partners loved her matter-of-fact approach.

Alan was a computer engineer who had worked for Marconi; he always knew about the latest technology, kept us on our toes, acted as a programmer and designer. Mauricette and Alan were older than the other researchers and once, when we were out for lunch together, we worked out that between the three of us, we had been married for 100 years. We thought that was wonderful, but one of the group at the table exclaimed, "That's awful; imagine staying with the same person for so long!" His remark quite upset me. Was it a generation thing or just him? Was there something wrong or unfashionable about being happily married? He wasn't one of my research group, I am pleased to say.

Not everyone in the group was as old as us. For example, George and I met when he was a first-year undergraduate and I'd been assigned as his personal tutor. He seemed to lose quite a bit of weight in his first term and, when I mentioned it, he said he hadn't been eating well – mainly tins of soup. George missed his mother's cooking and didn't know what to do himself. He had several (Greek) friends who were suffering in this way. A few weeks later I commented that he was looking much better, and he said, "Oh, we have met a wonderful Greek girl who is cooking for us". Really? I hoped she was being paid. George reassured me that they did return the favour.

George stayed on to do a master's degree with me, followed by a PhD, then became my Research Assistant and Teaching Fellow. I felt as if I'd adopted him. He worked hard and eventually took on leadership roles within the group. He learned to cook, too, and loved to bring in Greek dishes for us to try.

With Yin-Leng, on the other hand, I felt that she had adopted me, for she was always there on hand to help in any way she could – a very resourceful, fiercely independent person but kind and thoughtful at the same time. The students loved her no-nonsense, practical way of teaching programming and design skills. She too came to us through the master's programme, was employed as a research assistant and programmer on our research and regional development projects and completed her PhD with me.

The doctoral students were remarkable people; they had excelled in their own countries[95] and were being funded at great expense to study and live in Manchester. They came to join my team through mutual agreement, having submitted a research

[95] My postgrads came from Iran, China, Malaysia, Bahrain, Cyprus, Greece, Palestine, Canada, Nigeria.

proposal based on my interests as published on the university website: 'Human Computer Interaction, Co-operative Requirements Engineering and Facilitation'.

As well as individual supervisory meetings, we had Friday afternoon get-togethers when students would talk about their research, share references, discuss papers they were preparing and give each other feedback and encouragement. Their research shared themes such as 'trust': trust in e-commerce, trust in virtual teams, trust agents. Although each doctoral thesis has to be unique, it is important that it is positioned within a wider context. Initially some students found the idea of sharing difficult, wanting to 'protect' their own research. With gentle persuasion they slowly recognised how much their own work benefitted from the collaboration.

I encouraged the doctoral students to present their work at international conferences, invariably finding funds for travel and subsistence from my own research income or from the departmental allowance. I told them that a measure of a good PhD was to publish two conference papers and two journal papers and have a long list of future work. The more in-depth you go into a subject, the more you realise how little you know and how much there is still to do.

Many became involved in our e-Commerce events; it was good for their personal development to meet businesspeople and learn how to communicate their research to a more general audience.

The world of e-commerce and e-business was constantly changing.

The European Commission published a number of studies setting out their policies for the adoption of e-commerce and e-business by SMEs (Small to Medium Size Enterprises) across Europe [44]. They saw development within regions as key to economic growth, and set aside funds to stimulate take-up.

The vision was to create networked businesses throughout Europe. Successful businesses were already using internet technologies to communicate within their own organisation and between themselves and their partners. Increasingly, companies began to look again at how they were organised and to identify the key business processes that enabled them to operate. For example, processes within a major supermarket chain included finance, admin, purchasing, human resources, IT, distribution, warehousing and sales.

The fact that each of these processes was supported by IT, and that they could communicate with others via the internet, meant that they no longer needed to operate within a single organisational structure and could be outsourced to other organisations. For example, the supermarket chain could outsource distribution, warehousing and IT, and keep its core business of purchasing and selling goods in-house.

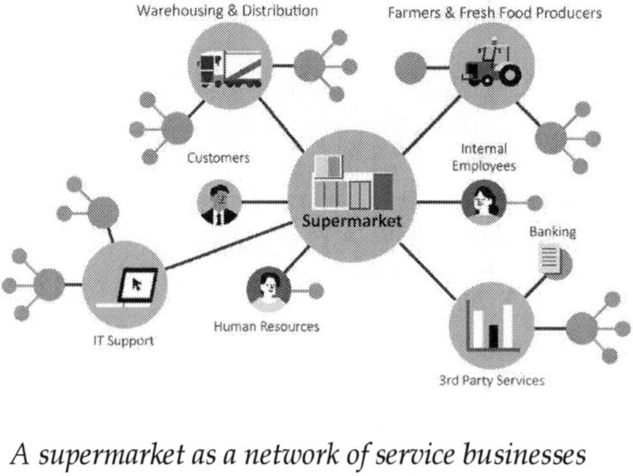

A supermarket as a network of service businesses communicating via the internet

Businesses began to ask, "What is my core capability, what do I need to do in-house and what can I outsource?" thus leading to the breakdown of a single organisation into a network of business functions.

I was keen to engage with this vision and see to what extent we could help SMEs in our region. We had already assisted individual SMEs, but here was an opportunity to help on a bigger scale.

Fortunately, one of our collaborators in the e-Commerce centre, Mark Stein, from Tameside Metropolitan Borough also saw the opportunity and asked if we would partner them in a funding bid to the European Regional Development Fund (ERDF). Our region of Greater Manchester had over 100,000 SMEs, rather too many for us to approach, but by focussing on one area where there was keen interest we had a chance to make a difference. We were successful in winning enough resources to reach out to the 6,000 SMEs in the Tameside area with the vision of creating networked organisations.

The university was supportive of our bid and agreed to contribute resources in kind to match the ERDF funds. The project administration was a nightmare but, thank goodness, we had Mauricette as our manager; it really did need her tenacity and attention to detail. She also had a great sense of humour and christened our project 'Graceland' saying it would make us smile and think of Elvis.

Tameside wasn't the most prosperous borough in Greater Manchester but it had the potential to benefit. Around half of the SMEs were in manufacturing, wholesale and retail, with others including construction, hotels, estate agents and financial intermediaries. In 2002, when the project started, there was generally a low uptake of internet technologies, with only 20% of businesses having a broadband connection and 30% having a website of any kind.

We worked alongside Tameside council staff to put on workshops and information evenings for the SMEs to explain the benefits of getting onto the internet and showing how they could apply for funding. Not everyone was keen, suggesting it was "just another imposition from Europe".

"I don't have time for this; I'm already working flat out."

"I don't see how this will benefit my business; I don't need to collaborate."

"More expense, I can't afford."

We felt an almost missionary zeal about the importance of these businesses coming to grips with the new technologies. We expected some resistance, but nothing would put us off.

We decided that the best way forward was to build a portal, that is, a software platform[96] on which an SME could create its own website simply by choosing pre-defined templates and completing forms. This would enable them to get online quickly without the expense of having their own specialist IT staff.

The portal also supported knowledge exchange and community building, with the aim of SMEs identifying others they might collaborate with, thus creating the beginnings of a networked business. One hope was that, by working together, they could bid for bigger contracts or respond to government tenders.

It was an uphill battle; despite the opportunities presented, there were too many obstacles in the way.

I felt we were witnessing the 'digital divide' in action.

Surely, it was obvious in the internet era that businesses should go online and take advantage of the connectivity to customers, suppliers and potential business partners that it would afford. There seemed to be a gulf between those who had ready access to computers and the internet and those who had

[96] The portal was built using readily available software: CSS, HTML and Javascript for the client side (user interface); Microsoft SQL for the database and Windows ASP for server-side scripting.

not. The digital divide wasn't just about technology; it was about education, expertise, resources and the confidence to try something new.

There was economic disadvantage in the borough; family incomes were low compared with the national average, and fewer than 50% of households owned a computer of any kind. Business owners were mostly drawn from the local population and few had benefitted from higher education.

Many complained that computers were difficult to use, which was not surprising as most applications (such as word processors, spreadsheets and databases) are complex and effective use assumes a high level of education. Many of the business owners were reluctant to participate in setting up the websites themselves, or learn the IT skills and had no staff to delegate to.

Of course, some businesses were entrepreneurial, built their websites and formed collaborations and embryonic networks, but these were in the minority. By the end of the project in 2004, we had around 400 active SMEs with six identifiable business networks. The service industries performed the best, often using a paid facilitator to manage the network for them [45].

Overall, the project had a measurable impact on only 6% of those targeted. If the same amount of effort had been expended elsewhere, in a more prosperous area of Manchester, such as Chorlton, probably we would have been more successful in creating networked businesses. However, the whole point of regional development funds was to bring those less active in the digital world up to the standard of the vanguard.

We did have individual successes and like to think that we at least added to the voices educating Tameside SMEs about the potential of the internet to support and extend their businesses.

It's important to remind those sitting in the ivory tower of the university that not everyone is like you and those around you. My colleagues, my research group, IT and most of the admin staff were graduates working in well-equipped offices, in receipt of regular training about new technologies, well-paid and motivated to learn.

We were most definitely on the other side of the digital divide.

This was just the beginning; not only did small businesses need to adopt the new technologies and learn to network and exchange services to survive, but they needed to be constantly embracing the opportunities of the internet era.

There were real worlds and virtual worlds hitherto unthought of.

Chapter 17 Living in a virtual world

One evening, early in 2008, I returned home from work and glanced at the television to see a long queue of people outside the Northern Rock bank. Savers were demanding their money. The bank had collapsed. It wasn't the only bank in trouble. Excessive risk-taking by US banks and the failure of Lehman Brothers highlighted the exposure of the British economy to global financial changes and the need for banking reform. The UK was about to suffer the deepest recession since the Second World War.

Everyone was affected. It became harder to obtain credit, house prices dropped and interest on savings was drastically reduced. We lost faith in traditional banks and looked to trusted supermarkets and ethical banks for greater transparency on how our money was being used.

Things were changing on the internet too. By 2008, the web had changed from a place where people viewed content in a passive manner to one that was much more interactive. Users could create content through blogs and wikis or communicate with each other through social media such as Facebook and Twitter and share videos through YouTube[97].

'Virtual Worlds' took interaction to the next level by visually recreating physical spaces in which a large number of people from different parts of the world could interact with virtual objects and with other people online, users being represented by virtual characters called 'avatars'.

Worlds were generally either game-oriented, for example, 'World of Warcraft', which is a fantasy, role-playing world, or socialisation-oriented, for example, 'Second Life', where the real world is recreated.

[97] Launch dates: Facebook 2004, YouTube 2005, Twitter 2006, World of Warcraft 2004, Second Life 2003.

My university had changed too; the UK government sought a reduction in the number of universities, and UMIST and the Victoria University of Manchester merged as a result. By 2007, amid major re-organisation, I found my research team reassigned to the Information Systems Group at Manchester Business School – a new office and new people to meet. The relocation didn't affect my research or teaching but it did open up new opportunities for collaboration. One of those was in Virtual Worlds.

The technology of 'Second Life' (SL) appealed to me because it had its own scripting language[98] which enabled users to build Virtual Worlds of their own. I was keen to learn more.

I needed people to help me explore, so I decided to invest one hour per week and invite colleagues to join me. We held a kind of jamming session where we could interact with each other and with Second Life without any particular purpose other than to please ourselves and learn along the way.

I let it be known, via email and word of mouth, that I was experimenting with SL, and if anyone wanted to join me they should come to my office at 12 noon on Fridays and bring a brown-bag lunch. My new office was relatively small, with room for four chairs in addition to my own desk and chair. Once word got around, the office was full – people sitting on the floor and standing in the doorway. I had an extra-large 60-inch television screen on a stand to one side of my desk; the screen was connected to my computer and displayed SL for all to see.

I never knew who was going to turn up, but if they brought their laptop they could log in to SL and our avatars could meet inside the virtual world and discover things together. Some came because they were interested in

---

[98] Linden Scripting Language (LSL) is largely based on programming languages Java and C.

psychology and wanted to understand the avatars and how they related to their owners. Some were software engineers who wanted to learn how to program using the LSL script. Others were interested in business and the potential for virtual-world commerce and trading in virtual goods. SL had its own currency, called 'Linden Dollars', which you could buy with real-world money. At first none of us knew what we were doing; we just enjoyed experimenting and learning from each other.

I remember my first visit into SL. I created an avatar of myself by choosing a female body, a European-looking face and short brown hair. My clothes were free - a brown jumper, blue skirt and flat shoes. I decided to call her 'LAM', essentially made up from my initials - not very imaginative. I bought some Linden Dollars as I'd heard there were shops in SL and I might want to buy something.

I had arranged to meet a colleague in the grounds of Stanford University. Stanford had built their own island in SL with a university library of virtual books that you could actually open and read.

I was surprised by how quickly I took on the persona of LAM, my avatar. I watched her via the screen and controlled her via the keyboard, but really felt that I was her.

This is the story of LAM's and my first experience:

....

LAM (or was it me) hated the unknown. Yet here she was, confronted by Daleks, dinosaurs and a man covered in chains. They looked at her, laughing because she was so obviously a newbie. Her plain skirt and jumper and regular hairstyle gave her away; she just took what she was offered on entry.

Where was she? There were mountains in the distance; she tried to walk along the pathway, but it kept disappearing below her. She was afraid, unsure; should she try to find a way out? She had agreed to meet her colleague in the grounds of the university, but how would she ever get there? Her colleague's avatar was called KT. LAM (or was it me) hated being late, letting KT down. Surely, if KT could find her way, then so could LAM.

Walking a little further LAM saw a map and decided that, if she just kept on walking and crossed a bridge, she would reach the university grounds. Odd 'people' and 'things' were all around her: a man with a huge poodle; a letter box that talked; flowers that swayed in the wind. Yet there was no wind. Just as she thought she was about to cross the bridge, she suddenly felt herself fall down and down into a crevasse, a dark, deep void. Her stomach (or was it mine) churned; everything was black, and she was lost as if in a nightmare.

Why had she agreed to come? It was too hard.

I remembered being told there were places like this in the virtual world, places which no-one had built, chasms between lands that no-one owned. (Press 'ctrl/s' to get back to land.)

Amazing! There she was in the university ground; she walked as fast as she could to find KT, even flying at one point. By flying she could see all around, and eventually she spotted KT sitting on a bench.

"Where have you been?" said KT.

"It's a long story, KT, but boy am I pleased to see you! I felt out of control and I hate that," LAM replied.

"What shall we do?" asked KT. 'I think by the look of you, we need to go shopping."

"Oh, yes please, I feel like everyone is staring at me."

KT replied, "I know a quick way to get to a shopping mall. Hit the menu and select 'designer mall239'."

At the mall LAM was delighted. She hadn't thought she would be so relieved to be shown how to navigate.

I was beginning to feel as though I was my avatar and was excited to be buying new clothes.

KT suggested an Armani suit, knowing that I liked to look smart.

"I'll never fit into that!" said LAM.

"Don't worry. When you put the suit on, your figure automatically takes on the shape of the suit," said KT reassuringly.

"Really, then I'll definitely have that."

It was a blue trouser suit, with a white shirt. The shape of her figure could be adjusted. LAM didn't want to look too sexy, but just have the waistline she'd always dreamed of.

"Next – shoes," KT said. "Did you know that shoes come with a walk? You can try them on and see which walk you feel comfortable with. You can strut or wiggle or be normal."

LAM was discovering herself. I'd never really been very interested in designer clothes but now felt really excited for LAM. I bought her a diamond bracelet that twinkled when she moved.

I felt irrationally happy that LAM was finding her way around and beginning to look like an SL resident, no longer a newbie.

……………………………………………

The clothes for my avatar cost only a few real-world pence. I was hooked; wondering what else could I buy? I met my younger daughter in SL and bought her avatar lots of new clothes together with a dog that nodded and made a purring sound when you stroked it. One day I bought a yacht and we went sailing on a lake.

I was beginning to find it difficult to disassociate my true self from my avatar. The more I customised my avatar the more it became part of my identity, and I found myself thinking about LAM even when I wasn't in SL.

Emboldened by the experimentation and interest among colleagues, the small group at our Friday jamming sessions decided that we wanted to build our own SL island for Manchester Business School for teaching and research. I put together a bid for funds to buy the land.

As luck would have it, my lobbying coincided with a visit to the Dean by a senior executive from IBM. She gave a presentation to the school in which she showed how IBM used virtual worlds within the company for meetups, conferences and giving demos to prospective customers. The Dean was captivated; it looked so exciting and, of course, being from IBM, very professional.

I was invited to join them for lunch and the Dean said to me, "You could do this for us Linda, couldn't you? Create a virtual business school?"

I responded enthusiastically and was delighted to be given the job. I knew it would be a lot of extra work and that it wasn't as easy as it looked. Our Friday lunchtime meetings turned into brainstorming sessions, exploring what we could do in SL that would actually be useful and justify the investment in time and money.

We thought, "This is a virtual world where we can do anything we like." There was no need to build a red-brick building like our real-world business school — no need for roofs or walls - we were unconstrained by real-world physics. Nonetheless, our avatars would have to find their way around, just like a normal website.

We decided on an impossible structure centred around a tower, with each level of the tower having 'rooms' coming off. Each level would be colour-coded, and the 'rooms' given names to make them easy to find. We wanted to reflect our Manchester industrial heritage and created cog-like entrance areas. The whole structure floated above blue water and was surrounded by blue skies.

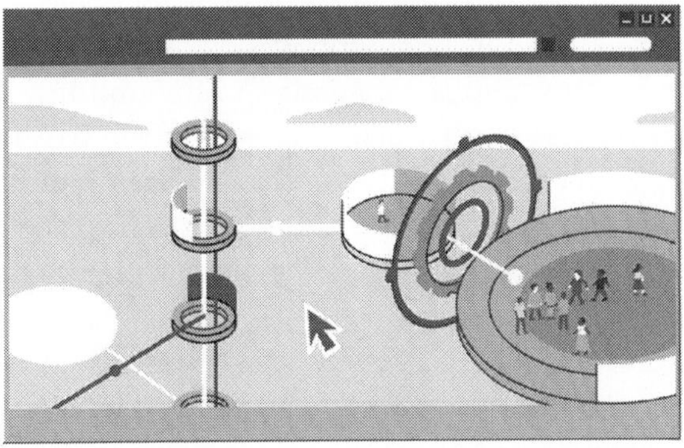

A view of Manchester Business School Second Life Island 2009

Like any project, we needed some 'quick wins' to convince others of the use of virtual worlds in education. Some colleagues used it to conduct research. One experimented with inworld medical consultations, another with teaching retail marketing students about shelf layout in a supermarket, and another with conducting opinion surveys related to new product design.

LAM made her SL debut at an event hosted by eSkillsUK. It was a careers fair for second-year students, with representatives from major companies giving talks in an SL-style lecture theatre and answering individual questions in virtual-world break-out rooms afterwards. Everyone joined from their own office, student lab or home - their physical location didn't matter, for they just had to transport their own avatar into the eSkillsUK Virtual World island. The students were briefed on what to wear and how to behave. I was nervous about the potential for chaos, knowing the range of costumes the students could turn up in. We created SL T-shirts with the Manchester Business School logo for all of them to wear, and in the event we had only a fleeting visit from a wizard and a Dalek that insisted on staying at the back of the lecture theatre.

Thankfully, LAM didn't have too much to do except simply introduce the eSkillsUK host who would chair the event.

Our activity with industry collaborators drew the attention of the Deputy Director for one of the Executive MBA programmes. His name was Doug and I'd seen him hovering in the doorway at a few of our Friday jams. The Exec MBA was already heavily supported by e-learning technologies and he could see the potential of SL.

His interest helped us achieve the 'quick win' we needed to raise enough funds to build a truly professional business school 'inworld'. We had bought the land and built a few rooms, but the rest was beyond the time available among our already busy schedules. This new investment allowed us to engage a software consultancy to build the impossible structure we dreamed of.

I was aghast when Doug suggested that SL be used for a graduation ceremony for the Executives on the BP Project Management programme.

"Our students are all senior executives holding critical roles; the current cohort are from Angola, Indonesia and Russia as well as the United States and Canada."

"Would they be willing to learn SL?" I asked.

"I think I could sell the idea," Doug reflected. "Previous students have complained about the difficulty of attending their graduation ceremony owing to the amount of time and travel involved in coming to Manchester."

I thought, "What is a graduation, why is it so important? For undergraduates it's a symbol of transition from one life stage to the next, from student to worker. It's also a ritual with set procedures, a procession, gowns, speeches, photographs, degree certificate."

"Doug, there's a lot involved in a graduation. The traditions go back centuries, it's a ritual, we'd have to keep with the current way of doing it," I said, cautiously.

"I agree, though we should be open too. Let's trial it." Doug was a good project manager.

"What about the dignitaries? The Dean of the Business School would have to be involved." I was thinking how the Dean would react when I asked to make an avatar of him.

"Yes, and the Pro-Vice-Chancellor and the Director of Projects for our sponsoring company," Doug replied.

"We need some serious thinking about how to do that – how to create their avatars, how to get them to walk in procession and to step on to the stage, and how they give speeches."

It all sounded rather daunting; none of us could find any precedent for this being done at any other university – a graduation in Second Life, this was new. We were fortunate to find a professional design agency to help us with this groundbreaking project[99].

We took a lead from IBM where their internal use of virtual worlds was strictly controlled. The Manchester Business School Island would only be accessible by invitation and would not be capable of being found by searching within SL. We also developed a code of conduct and dress code that participants had to adhere to, for otherwise they would be ejected from the Island.

This was official business.

Even LAM only got to attend the trial graduation to observe and comment on any improvements she could see from within the virtual world.

The ceremony [46] took place in two 'rooms' developed for this purpose in Second Life: a small ante-room where delegates and guests were welcomed on arrival and to which they returned to celebrate at the end of the award ceremony; and the main 'hall' where the actual ceremony was conducted - a

[99] Manchester Design Agency Corporation Pop led by Dom Raban https://corporationpop.co.uk/about accessed 27/02/22

virtual world Whitworth Room, (the Whitworth Room being where real-world graduations take place at Manchester University).

We created avatars for each graduate from photographs and provided gowns and a simple user guide describing how to move and interact but limited to essential information required to take part in the ceremony.

Custom made avatars of the Pro-Vice-Chancellor and the Director of Projects[100]

Speeches were pre-recorded; avatars and gowns, appropriate to the status of the dignitaries, were provided. During the ceremony, we brought in experienced operators for dignitary avatars, and a marching script to ensure that they marched in time during the procession.

[100] https://www.manchestereveningnews.co.uk/news/uk-news/virtual-graduation-ceremony-910609 accessed 27/02/22

Graduates received their certificates by a script-controlled handshake with the Pro-Vice- Chancellor. We made the event a memorable experience for participants by providing a souvenir inworld video of the occasion, downloadable certificates, and an opportunity for networking with fellow graduates.

Graduation ceremony - students listening to speeches by dignitaries

The first ceremony in February 2009 was successful and even got a write-up in the Financial Times. A second graduation was held in February 2010 and further events were scheduled.

The Dean and the Pro-Vice-Chancellor were particularly keen on the SL graduation because it meant they didn't need to attend each time for the ceremony. Their speeches were recorded, their avatars were controlled by scripts or by another person and they only needed to turn up for the celebration at the end.

I was surprised by how seriously the Exec MBA students took the whole ceremony; they all practised and were anxious that their avatars behaved as expected. They enjoyed the occasion and felt engaged, as evidenced by spontaneous celebratory behaviours at the end of the ceremony that mirrored those in 'real life', for example, throwing hats in the air and cheering.

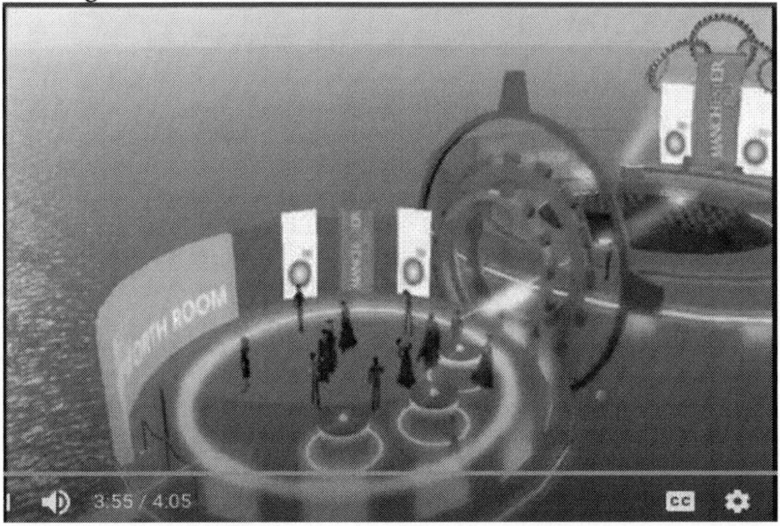

Graduates celebrating in the ante-room after the event

The graduates reported that they felt fully involved and that the ceremony and receipts of certificates seemed very real. Did they have as strong a relationship with their avatars as I did with mine? Research has shown that the more effort a participant makes in customising their avatar, the more they relate to their virtual-world identity. So, I think the answer is, probably, yes. [47].

The SL graduation was a success on many levels. The students had fun, a virtual-world graduation saved everyone time and money and we got our own MBS Island. Subsequently, LAM made many more appearances, giving tutorials to her own students, assessing teamworking and training teaching assistants how to facilitate student events inworld.

The experience of my digital persona LAM made me realise how easy it is to project an image of yourself in the virtual world, whether it be in Second Life or on social media. You can create an image and, in your own mind, become that persona.

Second Life challenges the boundary between real and virtual worlds. It enables residents to socialise, participate in group activities, and create and trade virtual products and services. SL's own currency (the Linden Dollar) can be converted into real-world dollars, thus creating a natural extension to the world of e-commerce, namely that of virtual-world commerce where digital goods and services are bought and sold by digital avatars.

I was beginning to wonder whether I was actually living in the virtual world.

It was fun to experiment with the new technology and to get something useful out of it. At the same time and with my feet firmly lodged on terra firma my research in e-commerce and e-business was continuing to evolve. The idea of businesses being part of a service ecosystem now supported the view of everything as a service. The paradigm was shifting and a whole new tranche of work developing. The field of Service Science was emerging and I was fully immersed with business, building communities and undertaking research, and even winning an award from IBM but there is too much to include here.

In the next chapter I reflect on my experience of leadership in the hope that others may learn from it.

Chapter 18 Just do it: be a leader

I never considered myself a feminist. In the 1970s, feminists were vociferous, active women like Germaine Greer. I empathised with her arguments about the submissive role of women in society but found her book 'The Female Eunuch' and the writings of other feminist theorists too abstract, and just lost patience with them.

In hindsight, I would describe myself as a 'get it done' sort of person. I wanted to live my life and achieve my ambitions regardless of my sex.

I strongly believe in equality: that all people should have an equal chance in life and equal opportunities to make progress.

I was 40 before I became fully aware of the challenges facing me as a woman. Up to this point, I'd been busy honing my expertise, gaining confidence in my abilities, having children, and understanding the demands of being a wife and mother while working full time. I knew I could achieve so much more in my career and that I had a flair for building teams, leading research projects and getting people on board with new ideas. I was always ready to take on a leadership role if it meant I could get things done.

Although many of the lessons I have learnt stem from my time in academia, I believe they can be applied in other domains and to all women, no matter what their age or profession. Here are seven of them.

Lesson one: Glass ceilings do exist

The term 'glass ceiling' is often used to refer to the invisible and unspoken barriers that confront women in their attempt to reach leadership positions, particularly where those positions are normally held by men. By 1995, the UMIST[101] Department of Computation had been in existence for over thirty years and up to that date all the professors and heads of department had been men.

I wanted to have a wider leadership role within the department and couldn't do that without first becoming a professor. There seemed to be invisible barriers; no-one was openly hostile but it was a new departure for them – a change in tradition - but neither was anyone offering to help me get promotion. I knew I had to be more strategic in my thinking and to lobby for support - to influence the opinions of the departmental professors and the Vice-Chancellor and those of external referees.

Was there a glass ceiling? I think so; no-one was saying 'join our club', and at least one of the departmental professors was against having a woman in their ranks.

[101] UMIST – University of Manchester Institute of Science and Technology 1964 until 2004 when it merged with The University of Manchester.

Once a professor I was in a position to become head of department and take on the wider leadership position I sought. Having broken through the glass ceiling, was I now heading for the 'glass cliff'?

The glass cliff refers to the phenomenon where women are over-represented in leadership positions that are risky or precarious. An example often cited [48] is that of Prime Minister Theresa May, who came to power immediately after the shock result, in 2016, of the UK referendum to exit the EU. A flurry of male politicians previously vying to become Prime Minister took a step back or step down – no-one wanted the job. Another example is that of Christine Lagarde, French Finance Minister, who took the lead at the International Monetary Fund at a time of crisis in 2011. In 2019 she went on to become the first female president of the European Central Bank. She is known for embracing 'glass cliff' situations and showing what a woman is capable of. [48]

"When the situation is difficult, when it's really challenging, when the financial situation is really poor, when budgets have been blown, then there are opportunities for women," says Lagarde. "I've always encouraged women to actually say yes in those situations. I have noticed, time and again, that when it's bad, you call women to the rescue. Or as a former central bank governor said to me… 'The men go to war, and the women pick up the pieces.'"[102]

I'm not comparing myself to these amazing women but feel I can still learn from them. The leadership position I sought was relatively small: a budget of £7million and around 70 staff. I wanted to be head of department because I could see so many problems that needed sorting out: grossly overworked staff, poor resourcing, and a lack of clear direction.

[102] https://qz.com/work/1658829/christine-lagarde-says-women-should-embrace-glass-cliffs-roles/
By Cassie Werber, July 4th, 2019. Accessed 27/01/22

I made it known that I wanted the position and even those departmental professors who had resisted my earlier promotion happily handed over the reins to me. Some professors had been head of department themselves and performed their duty. Others did not want the role: it would be far too much of an intrusion into their academic lives. They were keen for me to take over.

However, my position was risky; I could easily fail and end up with staff even more demoralised than they already were.

Having carefully watched the methods and behaviours of previous heads of department – all men of course – I was confident that I could learn from the best and do much better than the worst.

The lessons I learned about becoming a leader are:

If you want promotion and leadership, don't wait to be asked - devise a plan.

Stop being self-effacing; if you don't step forward, probably you will just be ignored.

Don't worry about the fact that you are a woman. Don't be put off by negative or sexist comments; just be confident in your own ability and do it anyway!

Don't give up!

Lesson two: Hone your negotiation skills

When I first started as head of department I thought 'I'm the boss, the staff have to do as I ask,' but it's more complex than that. They must want to do it…

Imagine this scene:

……………………………………………………………

I am head of department. C. is a senior academic. I need him to take on extra teaching over and above that required of his grade.

Me: "C, you know we are understaffed; I've called you in to ask for your help. Would you take over the teaching of the module on Privacy and Security?"

C doesn't exactly say NO, but: "This module is a waste of time".

I try to be direct and positive towards him: "It's in the syllabus and has to be taught and it's within your area of expertise."

C: "My work is undervalued by this department. This module is waffle; it needs to be more mathematical."

I think: 'What does he really mean? Is he undervalued? I know he can be an awkward customer, tends to plough his own furrow and doesn't mix much with the other staff. Do I need to make him feel valued? Maybe he just wants to include some of his own material on security?'

I try making a concession: "I'm sure there is scope for addition of your ideas within the overall objectives of the module. You can make some changes."

C: "The students just aren't up to it; their maths isn't good enough."

Where do I go from here? C's research is excellent, he genuinely is an expert in his field but has been passed by for promotion. Is this his real problem?

I can't let him walk out of my office without his agreeing to take on the module.

I try another tactic: you help me, and I'll help you.

"C, the next promotion round is coming up soon; let me work with you to prepare your case. Your recent paper in Lecture Notes in Computer Science was excellent and I'm sure will be very well received by the panel."

C: "Other Heads of Department have said they would help but never did."

Argh!

I smile at him and look him in the eye, lean slightly forward and move my head gently from side to side. "C, I'm not like other Heads of Department; you know how hard I've worked to get this position. I genuinely want to help you; you deserve promotion. Let's work together."

C looks down: "Just this once, I'll take the module, but I'm not doing it next year."

I'm thinking 'That's OK, I'll worry about next year when the time comes.'

"Thank you, C, I really appreciate your unique contribution to this department and your willingness to go the extra mile in these difficult times."

He has to have the last word: "...and I may or may not need your help with promotion. I have my own plans."

And I smile.

....

I came out of that encounter with what I wanted but had had to try several negotiating tactics to get him to agree. Experience has taught me that so much of leadership is about motivating other people and to be successful you need to make them feel valued.

Negotiation skills help deal with difficult people, get staff on side and also assist in dealings with your own superiors.

I learnt that no matter how good my negotiation skills, there was still room for improvement.

Lesson three: Having children

Women are expected to be good at everything both in their careers and in motherhood but increasingly realise they have a choice.

For me there is no greater gift than having a child and no greater responsibility than to raise them well. If you want a career and children, then you need a strong support network to ensure they are well cared for in your absence. You also need to be incredibly well organised. Time spent with family is precious and, no matter how busy you are, time with them should be written large in your diary. I learned to be strict about enforcing time with my children; to be in control of my schedule because no matter how old the child, they still need you.

In Julia Gillard's book 'Women and Leadership' [48] where she discusses work and family life with eight women leaders, she states: "Another lesson from our leaders is that there will be some guilt. Expect it and think how you will cope with it."

Other people can seemingly try to make you feel guilty, for example, saying to me, "Oh, you haven't brought your baby; don't you miss him, he is so young?" or, "How do the children feel about not seeing you for a week?"

How do I respond? I refuse to react, just smile. I know my children are being well cared for and that my family support my career choice. I simply want to be accepted as who I am and what I am capable of. My family life is no-one else's business.

Another lesson from Gillard's book is that leadership will not be forever; you step forward into the role for a period and then step back. A woman might think, "If I do it then it will take me away from my family forever. It won't." [48]

Why should a woman feel any more guilty than a man? A child has two parents who, assuming they are both able, have equal responsibility towards that child.

There has been very little discussion about the man being the primary carer for children, but maybe that will change.

Jacinda Ardern, the prime minister of New Zealand, who gave birth shortly after her appointment in 2017 said, "When we announced that Clarke (her partner) would be the primary care-giver, many women got in contact to explain that their husbands or partners had done the same thing. We haven't talked enough about that reversal of perceived roles. Why shouldn't we? Because these roles are for men as well. There should be no stigma attached to a man being primary care-giver."

I am very fortunate to have a supportive husband who – in the 1970s and 1980s – stayed at home to look after our three children when they were babies and toddlers. My mother, occasional paid help and neighbours helped to look after them when he went back to work full-time. It was useful to be part of the local community, school and church where we got to know who we could trust. The African proverb, 'It takes a village to raise a child' rings true.

Patrick and I had a network of support to help us raise the children, and I think I would have found it impossible to pursue a career otherwise.

Women I have mentored ask me: "Is it worth it?" referring to the struggle of juggling motherhood with a career. It can be incredibly difficult, especially where the job demands that they excel, and my experience is that to succeed women usually do have to achieve more than their male counterparts. Is it worth their constant tiredness, is it worth feeling guilty about not spending enough time with the children, is getting promotion worth all the hard work? There is no easy answer, in my view it's too exhausting for a woman to have sole responsibility for a child and work full-time, get promotion, and take on a leadership role. She needs a support network; she also needs to decide on her goals and devise a detailed plan for both home and work life. Above all she must be fiercely protective of her time, not taking on any tasks that don't fit with her goals.

Amazingly in 2020 almost 15% of women in the UK were sole parents.[103]

Even with a support network, somehow the overall responsibility for childcare seems to fall on the shoulders of the woman. Restrictions around the 2020 Covid-19 pandemic presented many families with the twin pressures of working from home and caring for children. Data shows duties within households mirrored ongoing gender divisions, with women doing more hours childcare than men, even when earning the same salary – 7 hours versus 4.5.[104]

I learned that pursuing an ambitious career requires focus, determination, planning, a strong support network and ideally a very supportive life partner who will share responsibility for children. Even then it will be incredibly hard work!

Lesson four: I am not an imposter

OK, so now I have that leadership position, am I up to it? I was wary of the imposter syndrome. Did I feel like an imposter, not able to live up to the expectations of others? Am I that woman who is afraid she will be found out at any moment? That, despite clear evidence of competence, she just doesn't deserve success.

Imagine this scenario: two women friends having lunch together in a bistro.

---

[103] UK Office for National Statistics. https://www.ons.gov.uk/peoplepopulationandcommunity/birthsdeathsandmarriages/families/bulletins/familiesandhouseholds/2020 accessed 27/01/22

[104] '"I feel like a 1950s housewife": How lockdown has exposed the gender divide', Donna Ferguson, The Observer, 3rd May 2020. https://www.theguardian.com/world/2020/may/03/i-feel-like-a-1950s-housewife-how-lockdown-has-exposed-the-gender-divide accessed 27/01/22

....

The conversation:

"Congratulations, you did so well to get that promotion, you must be so-o-o excited."

"Excited? Yes, I am, but terrified at the same time."

"Why are you terrified? It's the perfect job for you. You'll be amazing."

"My mum always said I'd get my comeuppance one day. She says I'm too ambitious and will overstretch myself. I think she might be right; I've done it this time. I know I won't be able to do this job."

"Of course you can."

"Mum always said I was too 'bossy'. You all think I'm good but, deep down, I know I'm not. I'm a fraud, an imposter, I should never have applied for a leadership position. Me lead? Ha! That is a joke; why would anyone follow me? I'm so wishy-washy. I can't make decisions."

"Come on – you are too hard on yourself. Never mind your mum; I'm sure she'll be proud of you. What about your dad; he'll be pleased, won't he?"

"Dad – he's so wrapped up in his own job – did you know he's a minister of state now. Nothing I do will ever be good enough for him. I wish I'd never applied to lead the group; others are so much better than me."

"Look, just relax, think about all the things you are good at; you don't have to please your parents any more, you are a full-grown woman, have confidence! There really is something to celebrate."

....

Are her doubts real or imagined? Is this 'imposter syndrome'?

Whatever the situation, such negative thoughts can be debilitating. If I had any doubts, I had to work to overcome them. Get to know myself, ME as I am NOW.

I realise that being a leader can test everything about you; if people want to get at you or resist your leadership, they will try every angle to undermine you. I knew I mustn't let them, not doubt myself; build my inner strength and a deep belief in myself.

I spent time thinking about myself and trying to analyse how to strengthen my self-confidence.

I thought about my background: what was it that made me want to achieve what I have, and deep down, what motivates me, what are my values? I listed my strengths and weaknesses, how I could build on my strengths and what or who could complement my weaknesses. I tried to be clear in my own mind why I wanted the job and what I hoped to achieve for the department and as a leader. I thought about the amount of work and physical stamina I would need and was determined to build my physical fitness.

In chapter 14 I discussed leadership styles. I felt it was important to choose a leadership style that would suit my values and my personality. A mix of authoritative and facilitative leadership style would be best, leading from the front while, at the same time, allowing staff to contribute, empowering them to grow and develop as individuals. My aim was to give them a sense of ownership and direction within their own groups and energise them into contributing to the department as a whole.

Gillard observes: "Women leaders need to walk a tightrope between being seen to have authority while not being seen to lack empathy and nurturing skills." [48]

This was a new challenge; I had to embrace any fear and use it to build my competencies in the role, be positive about myself, kind to myself, and choose a leadership style that suits me.

Lesson five: Keeping the sharks at bay

I'm a great believer in job satisfaction: that if individuals are happy at work, then much more can be achieved collectively. Through listening, I learned that there were many reasons why people might be dissatisfied and felt privileged if, as head of department, I could change things for the better.

To quote Michelle Obama [49]: "Success isn't how much *money* you make, it's about the *difference* you make in people's lives."

I also believe that people need to feel in control and are happier if they have clearly defined tasks that they can take ownership of. I learned to assess the extent to which I could delegate and trust staff to get on with it. Some were very effective when given a wide remit with little supervision while others needed highly defined tasks with frequent oversight. I tried to build an atmosphere of mutual trust.

Of course, getting your former peers onboard is one thing but getting your new peers (the professors) on board quite another. You might think that because you have been given the leadership position your peers would just let you get on with it, but no, they still have opinions. They may snipe at you from the sidelines or openly oppose you in meetings.

Even Prime Ministers are only as powerful as their cabinet allows them to be. *"We are always fundamentally in a position where if cabinet ministers wish to assert themselves then the power of the Prime Minister will be checked and balanced in that way."*[105]

In my case, 'the cabinet' was the Committee of Professors. They were my peers and had recommended my appointment to the Vice-Chancellor. The Committee met twice a year to review departmental matters. As head of department I chaired the meeting and set the agenda.

It seemed as though I was in control throughout the first year of leadership but, in the second year, I found myself being openly opposed. Here is an extract from one such meeting:

Me: "Item 3.2: Redistribution of Research Funds. You can see from the paper circulated with the agenda that I am proposing a change to the distribution of department research monies. Under the current system a share goes to each of you as professors and then you allocate it to academics in your research group as you think fit ..."

Prof X interrupted: "I'm sorry, Linda. I have to stop you there. I veto this item."

Me: "Pardon, Veto?"

Prof X: "Yes. There can be no further discussion of this item."

I looked towards the other profs for support, but they just shrugged their shoulders.

It was like hitting a brick wall. I didn't even know that the power of veto existed in these meetings, but it did, and he had invoked it. He informed me that a veto meant there was to be no further discussion on the matter and so I was prevented from negotiating my way to a compromise solution.

---

[105] The Role and Powers of Prime Ministers.
[a note from the House of Lords Select Committee on the Constitution 2010: 12]

I had discussed the proposal with some of the professors before the meeting but not all, not X. I'd had a generally positive reaction, so I thought it was worth putting the proposal on the table.

The existing system of allocating research funds was archaic: giving a professor power over the academics in his group. Professors could demand favours in return for funds, for example, insisting that his name be added to the list of authors on the research paper. Some academics might choose not to go to a conference rather than have to ask for money and be indebted to him.

My proposal was to share departmental research monies equally among the academic staff, bypassing the professors and consequently taking away some of their power and status.

What should I do?

Did I give up? No. I thought, 'There will be other ways and other times I can change this unfair situation. I just need to go away and think, and consult privately with my mentor.'

I continued to lobby the professors and discuss the proposal more openly with the academics. Eventually, everyone had the expectation that it was going to happen; it just built momentum and the next time I tabled the proposal, even Prof. X had to accept it.

This is just an example, but the overall lesson for me is that you are the leader because your peers and superiors want to you be, but you have to work hard to keep them on board. You may have your own goals, your own agenda, but just because you are in a leadership position, it doesn't mean you can automatically accomplish what you want.

Lesson six: Mentoring is good

The first time I was asked to be a mentor was in the late 1990s when I received a call from Human Resources (HR) asking if I would mentor a young lecturer from the Engineering Department. The lecturer had been complaining about unfair treatment by her head of department and HR thought I could help her deal with the situation. I'd had no formal training as a mentor but felt I could at least offer her a listening ear and empathy much needed when you have a problem.

Her name was Jen and as she entered my office I saw a petite young woman, maybe 28 or 30, with long, brown hair loosely tied back and a rather weary look on her face. I invited her to sit down and offered a glass of water; she looked like she needed a rest.

After introducing myself Jen told me her doctorate was in aeronautical engineering and that she had been appointed as lecturer to join a team of specialists in the department. The conversation started with me asking if she enjoyed her work.

"In principle, yes, I do enjoy the work, but I had expected much more flexibility."

"Flexibility? In what way – tell me more."

"I have a young child, two years old. She goes to the campus nursery, so I expected to be able to fit my work around that and work evenings or weekends if I needed to."

"I see, that sounds reasonable."

"Unfortunately, my head of department is insisting that I work in my departmental office from 9am to 5pm from Monday to Friday. He comes down at random times of the day to check that I am there and sends me an email complaining if he can't find me."

I didn't know her head of department (HoD), nor anything much about her department.

"Really – does he do this with all the staff?"

"No that's my problem, he doesn't."

"What about the other female academics?"

"I am the only one, and this is the first time a woman has been appointed."

Her HoD was out of line, because it was the norm in the university for academics to manage their own time. Was he being deliberately sexist, did he just have no understanding or was he worried that employing a woman was a risk? As much as his behaviour annoyed me, I was Jen's mentor and must focus on her. How could she deal with the situation? I felt it was my role to help her achieve her goals, not to intervene between her and her boss.

"Jen, this is clearly an untenable situation. As a mother myself, I know how hard it is to balance work and home. Children don't always stick to a schedule. You need flexibility in how you manage your time."

"Yes, but what can I do?"

"Let's explore some options. Have you tried speaking directly to him?"

"Yes, but he just talks down to me – says he knows best and that it's for my own good."

"OK, so why not just ignore him? You won't be the first."

"I'm in the first year of a three-year probation period and I need this job – I can't afford to get a bad assessment."

"A bad assessment? I've never heard of anyone failing probation for their timekeeping. The tenure panel are primarily concerned with your research output and teaching performance."

"I'm not sure how it works."

"I think there are a couple of things we could work on together. Firstly, I have guided numerous academics through the probation process and if we agree to meet regularly, I can guide you too. I can help you build your tenure profile. What do you think?"

"Thank you, though I know my research is good."

"Excellent. Now, regarding flexibility, maybe there is a middle ground. We academics have so many demands on our time; to be successful we have to make choices about what we do and how much time we allocate to it. For example, a colleague of mine, a young woman with a child like yourself, decided to limit how many meetings she would attend. She attended one in three. This was enough for her to be seen as contributing and freed up hours of her time. A smart move that

worked very well. She always spoke out at the meetings that she did attend to be sure she was noticed."

"I see."

"Yes, it's about being strategic. How many meetings can you miss without it being noticed too much? How many times can you be out of your office without too much comment? There has to be a middle ground. It's not all or nothing – and you have to draw the boundaries yourself. You have to be in control of your own schedule. You need to spend as much time as you can on research because that will get you tenure."

"Yes, that sounds good. My life is so stressful; everyone is making demands. I don't feel in control."

"OK. Let's jot down a few actions and agree to meet again – maybe weekly until we figure out how to solve this problem."

Did I go too far for a first meeting? Or maybe not far enough? Had I been listening properly? Jen's starting point was her HoD expecting her to be in the office all the time, but she was afraid to say no because of perceived consequences. I had tried to tackle the 'perceived consequences' and to give her a strategy that would help dispel her fears. Was I right? Did I give the right advice? Only time would tell. I felt that she also needed a way of dealing with the intrusive HoD. I needed to get to know her better.

Typically, mentoring is a longer-term activity where the mentor supports, advises and guides the mentee. After the initial session, the mentee is expected to drive the meetings, ideally focussing on one topic at each meeting, and working to achieve specific personal development goals. The mentor listens and advises, based on personal experience. The conversation is private and, ideally, a trusting relationship develops between the two parties.

With Jen, it took a while to build trust. She had been to HR initially to complain about the inflexibility of her HoD. HR came to the conclusion that it was she that needed mentoring rather than her HoD who needed to change his ways. I felt, and I think she felt too, that the onus to sort out the problem was being placed on her, rather than on him.

Nonetheless, as a mentor I felt I had a lot to offer in terms of advising Jen, both in her career development and the life skills needed to cope with the many demands on her time.

Many organisations, including the university, now have formal mentoring schemes with training for both mentor and mentees. Marks and Spencer use artificial intelligence techniques for matching mentors and mentees from across the whole business.[106] Some reach out beyond organisational boundaries.

I was fortunate to benefit from one such scheme myself. I was already a professor, in a senior role, when a contact from IBM suggested I might join their mentoring programme as a mentee. My mentor was an IBM Distinguished Engineer, a man with experience in a number of roles within the company and with a track record of innovation, a host of contacts and knew how to get things done.

We occasionally met face-to-face but mostly conducted our meetings online. I found it most helpful to have someone to talk to about seemingly intractable problems. The fact that he was from a different organisation meant he brought new and refreshing perspectives. He was interested in the direction of my research and introduced me to staff within IBM, in many ways going beyond being a mentor to becoming a sponsor.

Being a mentor myself helped affirm my own confidence while at the same time help others. I also learned that you are never too young, too old or too senior to have a mentor; there are always benefits in being listened to and advised by someone with more experience.

---

[106] M&S corporate mentoring scheme https://corporate.marksandspencer.com/stories/blog/making-the-perfect-match-how-we-re-using-data-to-revitalise-our-mentoring-scheme accessed 27/01/22

Lesson seven: Learning to be myself

Leadership takes many forms; you don't have to be a Prime Minister or head of a large corporation to be a leader. For example, leading a community garden group, organising food delivery for those in need, leading a school choir, supervising children's groups – whether neighbourly or grandiose; there are always opportunities to be a leader.

It may seem that leadership is hard work; it can be of course, but I have found it to have many rewards and be a source of joy in my life.

One question I've learnt to ask myself is Why? Why do you want the leadership role? What is your vision? In what way do you want to make a difference?

Is it a desire for more money, a mission to achieve something, a desire to improve people's lives, to run the company according to your style and values, to right the wrongs you see around you every day, introduce innovations into the workplace, be part of the decision-making team, become a c-suite executive? Whatever the answer to the question Why? - keep focussed on that, you must stay true to yourself and make a plan.

I found that having a plan was crucial - setting out what I wanted to achieve within six months, within a year, in three years then constantly re-evaluating the plan and measuring my actions against it. The very act of deciding I wanted a leadership role caused me to re-assess my everyday activities and change my mind-set.

Role models are important and I may aspire to be like one of them but, ultimately, they are not me. I found it important to get to know myself, articulate my values, identify what I was prepared to change and what must remain constant. According to a Guider book report[107] women leaders excel at: being honest and ethical, providing fair pay and good benefits, giving guidance and mentorship and being a spokesperson for the company. I wanted all of the above and at the same time to be technically excellent in my chosen field. Above all, I would prefer not to be judged as a 'female leader' but simply as a 'leader'. A leader and a woman in tech.

To quote Sheryl Sandberg [50], Chief Operating Officer (COO) of Facebook:

"The word 'female,' when inserted in front of something, is always with a note of surprise. Female COO, female pilot, female surgeon — as if the gender implies surprise ... One day there won't be female leaders. There will just be leaders." [108]

However, there will never be more leaders if we don't get more women in tech - the next chapter discusses why this is so important.

107 https://www.guider-ai.com/resources Guiderbook: Facilitating Female Leadership, accessed 27/01/22

108 https://www.womenintech.co.uk/5-powerful-quotes-by-women-in-tech accessed 27/01/22

Chapter 19 Who codes matters

In the spring of 2015, Louise Selby, a paediatrician, joined the gym close to her place of work in Cambridge, UK. To her surprise, she was denied access to the women's locker room and, no matter how often she swiped her card, the system wouldn't authorise entry. Naturally, she complained.

On investigation, the gym owner, PureGym, found that the third-party software it used to manage membership data was relying on members' titles to determine which locker room they could access. [51]

The title 'Doctor' was coded as male.

How did Dr Selby feel when she was denied entry? Probably extremely annoyed. She had signed up to the gym, paid her fee and arrived ready to do a workout only to find she could not access the changing room. She had to complain at the desk, then to the manager and escalate the problem until someone discovered that 'doctor' was not considered to be a valid title for a woman. I wonder how many more doctors who happen to be women were denied access and had to complain.

It appeared to be a simple programming error. The logic of the program on the door entry system was probably a simple IF…THEN…ELSE statement.

On the women's locker room it would be

IF title = <miss, mrs, ms> THEN open door ELSE show red light

and on the door of the men's locker

IF title = <mr, master, doctor> THEN open door ELSE show red light.

One or two lines of code.

You must ask why the person who wrote the code didn't include 'doctor' for the women's locker room. Was it unconscious bias?

This example illustrates how easy it is for bias to be programmed into a computer and in this case, it was replicated in all 90 locations of the gym across England.

It also highlights how easily outdated views can be encoded into a system. Someone decided that 'doctor' be coded as male; maybe they were just lazy or had never encountered a female doctor.

Did anyone consult women in the specification of the code or once the code was in place? Was the swipe card tested to see if it worked as intended? Participation by a more diverse group of people in the specification and design would soon discover that 'member title' is not a good determinant of locker room access rights.

In fact, the problem goes deeper: it's not just a question of what is in the code, but it's how that reflects what happens in the real world – it should reflect present-day cultural and ethical values. For example, some members may prefer gender-neutral changing rooms and find the simple binary choice of male or female unacceptable.

Technology is not neutral; what is written in code has an impact on real lives.

It is important that we understand how programs come into being and are able to question the underlying assumptions.

If software can be designed in a way which results in bias *against* women, it can also be designed with bias *towards* women.

Recovering from her experiences of sexual harassment at the dating app company Tinder, Whitney Wolfe[109] decided to develop a dating app of her own with a distinctly female bias. A major part of her mission for the new app 'Bumble' was "to counter misogyny and re-write archaic gender roles".

---

[109] https://edition.cnn.com/2019/12/13/tech/whitney-wolfe-herd-bumble-risk-takers/index.html Accessed 30/01/2022

For example, she became particularly interested in helping women in India where, in 2018, despite rising levels of education, gender awareness and stringent pro-women laws, violence against women was increasing[110]. Her company listened to the women of India and conducted surveys and focus groups to find out what problems they faced, their attitudes towards dating apps and the kind of features they would find helpful.

Whitney Wolfe saw Bumble as an opportunity to empower women, and introduced safety precautions. Built into the design was a feature whereby women always make the first move, hence reducing unwanted attention from men they don't consider suitable. Women can select men but not vice versa. Women also have the choice to display a first initial, rather than a full name. Keeping their name secret helps reduce their concerns about men seeking them out and stalking them.

Changing the design from both sexes being able to make the first selection to only women signals a change in the traditional gender roles where men always make the first move.

Bumble also recruits staff from a wide range of backgrounds, thus encouraging a cross-section of views within the design process: they 'strongly encourage people of colour, lesbian, gay, bisexual, transgender, queer and non-binary people, veterans, and individuals with disabilities to apply'[111].

Technology is not neutral; bias can easily be built into the code, either unintentionally, as in the case of PureGym, or deliberately, as in Bumble.

Everyone is biased in some way, so if software is specified and designed primarily by one section of society then it will

---

[110] https://www.theguardian.com/commentisfree/2018/apr/27/india-abuse-women-human-rights-rape-girls accessed 11/05/2021

[111] https://thebeehive.bumble.com/careers/ accessed 11/05/2021

reflect their bias. Technology is too important to all our lives for this glaring problem to be left unchallenged.

If one line of code can embed cultural assumptions ('doctor' is a male title), then what about programs that contain many lines of code, such as algorithms? Do we know enough to challenge their assumptions, or do we just have blind faith in the computer and its programmers?

I first came across the term 'algorithm' in 1972 when writing paging algorithms as part of my master's degree. They are much more straightforward than you might think and if you engage with any kind of digital service you will be using them.

An algorithm is simply a list of instructions to the computer, a number of lines of code setting out some procedure for the computer to follow. They are constructed by humans, are direct and unambiguous, and are capable of being tested. In other words, the human can test whether the outcome from the algorithm is the one they intended – and, if not, then correct the instructions until the intended outcome is achieved.

If you use the web or social media, algorithms will be supporting you all the time. The most straightforward are rule-based and do everyday tasks like prioritising, classifying, finding associations and filtering. Facebook and Twitter, for example, use filtering algorithms to remove information and isolate what is important. They filter stories that relate to your known interests to design your own personal feed.

When you search on Google, a prioritisation algorithm will try to predict the page you are looking for by making an ordered list and prioritising the entries according to the words you have entered and other known data such as your location or what you have searched for in the past.

Dating apps look for points of connection between members and suggest matches based on the findings. They use association algorithms to find links and make relationships between items of data.

These examples use data you input yourself or data garnered about you from other sources and most applications will use a combination of algorithms.

You are never far from an algorithm; they are monitoring you and collecting data whenever you or your gadgets are online. Data from cookies running on your computer are fed through classification algorithms to classify you based on your interests and characteristics which then provides valuable information for advertisers.

Rule-based algorithms can only be written if humans understand the problem and know how to write the instructions.

"In theory anyone can open them up and follow the logic of what's happening inside." [52]

Not many people even try to 'open up' the algorithm and discover what the rules are; what data is collected about them or how decisions are made, let alone the cultural assumptions underlying the rules. The algorithm is wrongly treated as a 'black box'.

Algorithms today have gone from mathematical abstractions to powerful mediators of everyday life, making our lives more efficient, more entertaining and better informed. However, allegedly anonymised datasets routinely leak our most sensitive personal information: statistical models for everything from mortgages to college admissions reflect racial and gender bias. [53]

Cathy O'Neil, in her book 'Weapons of Math destruction' [54], reiterates that a fundamental problem with many algorithmic systems is their reliance on historical data. "Big data processes codify the past, they do not invent the future." If the past was biased, then these systems will keep that bias alive.

Having said that, it is not just the data collected that matters it is also the inferences that can be made from the data that is potentially problematic. Kearns and Roth [53] cite an example where in 2018 the New York Times obtained a commercial dataset containing location information collected from iPhone apps. Such datasets contain precise locations of hundreds of millions of individuals. While superficially anonymous, without names attached, the data does track every move of each individual. For example:

'...from this data the New York Times was able to identify a forty-six-year-old math teacher named Lisa Magrin. She was the only person with a daily commute from her home in upstate New York to the middle school where she works, fourteen miles away. And once someone's identity is uncovered in this way, it's possible to learn a lot more about them. The Times followed Lisa's data trail to Weight Watchers, to a dermatologist's office, and to her ex-boyfriend's home. She found this disturbing and told the Times why: "It's the thought of people finding out those intimate details about you that you don't want them to know..."' [53]

Lisa was told what the data was revealing about her but we can all be subject to the same kind of data analysis and never know. Widely available data sets can be used to make decisions about our lives and don't seem to have any limits on the use of the data or algorithms. While laws and regulations need to be in place we also need better methods for the design of algorithms. People should be placed at the centre of design and algorithms should encode the ethical principles of society - the ethical algorithm. [53]

Virginia Eubanks in her book Automating Inequality [55] suggests that data scientists, systems engineers and hackers follow principles of non-harm: akin to a Hippocratic Oath which includes:

'I will integrate systems for the needs of people, not data

I will choose system integration as a mechanism to attain human needs, not to facilitate ubiquitous surveillance

I will not collect data for data's sake, nor keep it just because I can

When informed consent and design convenience come into conflict, informed consent will always prevail

I will remember that the technologies I design are not aimed at data points, probabilities or patterns, but at human beings' p213

"We want the world to remember that who codes matters, how we code matters and that we can code a better future." – Algorithmic Justice League[112].

[112] Algorithmic Justice League https://www.ajl.org/about accessed 11/05/2021

Chapter 20 Becoming a woman in tech

I found it quite alarming that at the beginning of 2020 only 16% of the IT professional workforce were women [56]. Despite national conversations about gender diversity, women in the tech industry are still under-represented, underpaid and often discriminated against.

The hard truths of an uphill battle still exist. [57]

Why is this?

Some argue that there are biological and psychological differences between men and women that make women unsuitable for a career in tech. For example, James Damore, software engineer at Google, has implied that women's 'stronger interest in people' and their 'neuroticism' might make them naturally less suited to being coders. [58]

This view may seem extreme but, given that only 23% of Google engineers are women, (a figure matched by Facebook, Apple and Microsoft [59]), it may be that Damore had little actual experience of technical women at work and simply based his view on some preconception or unconscious bias. Whilst he may sound extreme, he could well be voicing an opinion that others wouldn't.

Refuting Damore's claim, Prof Dame Wendy Hall, Director of the Web Science Institute at the University of Southampton, points to the wide variation in gender ratios internationally. She states that "While only 16% of computer science undergraduates in the UK are female, the balance is different in India, Malaysia and Nigeria (nearer 50%)" and goes on to argue that variation "would not be seen if there were universal basic difference in ability between sexes". [58]

In fact, Prof Gina Rippon, a neuroscientist at Aston University, Birmingham, has studied cognitive differences between men and women and points out that, in many cases, differences between male and female performance are very small and can disappear altogether with training. [60]

If women are not innately unsuitable for tech, then what exactly is the problem?

The first programmers were women - the human "computers" who performed complex calculations for the military during the second world war. These jobs were considered menial, akin to typists and considered women's work. Mathematical programming by women in the 1960s, for example for the first Apollo Space mission [61], brought computing to the fore. As the industry grew more lucrative, jobs became higher-status and better-paid, and it became more popular with men.

By the 1970s, computer companies were rapidly expanding, and aptitude tests were used to assist with staff recruitment. Tests were developed using the existing, predominately male population and consequently tended to reinforce their characteristics – typically eliminating extroverts and those who have empathy for others, whilst being biased towards nerdy, 'head in the machine' engineers.

It was a cycle: the hiring process favoured men, so men became over-represented in technology companies and fed popular perceptions of tech as a masculine domain.

By the 1980s women were already under-represented.

In the 1980s and 1990s home computers were mostly to be seen in the boys' bedroom and often the object of father-son bonding. In the 90s a study of hundreds of computer science students at Carnegie Mellon University by psychologist Jane Margolis revealed that 'There was a cultural assumption that the norms of being in computer science were that you would do it 24/7, were obsessed with it, wanted nothing in your life but computers – and that was very much associated with male adolescents. Females were made to think that, if they didn't dream in code and if it wasn't their full obsession, they didn't belong or were not capable of being in the field.' [62]

These attitudes lingered and have influenced parents over the decades, many asking whether computer science is an appropriate subject for their daughters to study.

RECRUITMENT

So why is there still a problem? Is it about recruitment?

At interview, young women are often reticent in speaking out about their expertise. In my experience, where a man might claim he can do everything on the checklist, a woman might focus on a few skills and abilities and be too quick to admit her shortcomings. A number of companies I encountered addressed this problem by changing their interview process, asking candidates to carry out problem-solving tasks and to write actual programs. They claimed it led to more female recruits. So apparently, a process that encourages women to show what they can actually do, rather than talking about it, works in their favour.

Some employers when recruiting still see a young woman's potential for pregnancy and maternity as problematic[113]. The campus-style culture that encourages workers to be on site from dawn to dusk can put women off as it can be hard for a primary carer to be 'part of the team'.

RETENTION

Young women who decide to take a career break to look after the children find it incredibly difficult to get back into the fast-moving world of tech. I witnessed some of their problems myself when mentoring on a series of courses for women

---

113

https://assets.publishing.service.gov.uk/government/uploads/system/uploads/attachment_data/file/465930/BIS-15-447-pregnancy-and-maternity-related-discrimination-and-disadvantage.pdf accessed 8th September 2021

returners. Some had been away for ten years from 2003 to 2013, raising several children, during which time the technology and programming languages had changed radically. We taught some of the same techniques we were teaching school children – using HTML/CSS for making websites and Python for more technical programming. The six-week courses were funded by the European Social Fund in recognition of the need to recruit and retain more women. Longer maternity leave, men taking their fair share of responsibility and better nursery provision also help with retention. Some companies now offer 'returnships' for more senior women, supporting them to get up to speed quickly after maternity leave.

SEXISM

It doesn't help recruitment of young women when, in 2021, despite some amazing role models, many of those working in tech still experience discrimination and report that their gender has made it harder for them to succeed.[114]

Some have spoken out leading to claims for sexual harassment or illegal discrimination against their employer, for example at Uber and Tinder. In 2014, the dating app Tinder was sued by the company's co-founder Whitney Wolfe[115] for 'atrocious sexual harassment and sex discrimination'. She accused the Chief Marketing Officer, Justin Mateen, of repeatedly calling her a 'slut' and a 'whore'. She alleged that he told her she made the company 'look like a joke' as a '24-year-old girl with little experience' and that he said that 'Facebook and Snapchat don't have girl-founders. It just makes Tinder look like an accident'.

---

[114] https://www.womenintech.co.uk/small-amount-of-women-in-stem. Accessed 30/01/22

[115] https://edition.cnn.com/2019/12/13/tech/whitney-wolfe-herd-bumble-risk-takers/index.html Accessed 30/01/22

Was it really her age he objected to as much as the fact she was a 'girl'? Zuckerberg was 19 when he founded Facebook. Spiegel, Murphy and Brown were still students in their early 20s at Stanford University when they founded Snapchat. Whitney Wolfe won her case and later became founder and CEO of the exceptionally successful dating app Bumble[116] and now encourages other women through her book 'Make the First Move'. [63]

At Uber, where in 2017, 85% of technical employees were male, one engineer, Susan Fowler, wrote a tell-all blogpost that revealed a workplace where managers propositioned female employees for sex whilst human resources (HR) did little to stop it. She reported receiving inappropriate emails and was told by HR that this was a first offence and that the male perpetrator was a 'high performer'[117], implying that she shouldn't rock the boat. Fowler later found out that HR were saying exactly the same to other women who complained. By the time she resigned the number of female staff had fallen from 15% to only 3%. [64]

These are powerful women who have spoken out and their experiences do nothing to help with recruitment let alone retention of women in computing.

In her 2020 book, Uncanny Valley, Anna Wiener tells of her experience of working in Silicon Valley: "It is an industry birthing billionaires, influencing not just how we behave but also the health of our democracies and the direction of our politics." [65] Her experience tells us to be wary. "The engineers might look like geniuses, but they are naive young men who hire in their own image in the apparent belief that they have some magic money-making ingredient not shared by the rest of

---

[116] https://bumble.com/en/about Accessed 30/01/22

[117] https://www.susanjfowler.com/blog/2017/2/19/reflecting-on-one-very-strange-year-at-uber Accessed 30/01/22

us." Wiener goes further: "They have fostered a narrow culture so incapable of self-reflection, empathy or humility that only disaster can follow."

Major change is needed to allow women to participate fully. The problem is down to issues inherent in the overall system, including attitudes, culture, sexism and lack of insight.

"As we go into the world of AI, when people are designing algorithms that help us live our lives, it will be very bad if that's all done by men. Social care, looking after kids, so many aspects of our lives.

We really need as many people as possible doing this. It's really important and it's going to get more important." Wendy Hall [66]

STARTING YOUNG

Early in the 21st century, activities designed to change attitudes were introduced in schools and in the community. By 2010, a national initiative of Code Clubs[118] was in full swing. I led a club myself for 8- to 10-year-olds in a local primary school. I met weekly with a dozen or so boys and girls to teach coding, using Scratch[119]; it was the perfect age to start - the children were fluent at reading and able to follow instructions. We mostly stuck to the graded exercises provided by Code Club and created interactive games to help them learn the main programming constructs. Once they reached a certain level I encouraged them to design their own games. The children showcased their work at the school assembly, and in this way, we sought to educate teachers and parents about computers.

I managed to keep equal numbers of boys and girls most of the time. They were all so eager to learn and excited by the immediate feedback of seeing their programs actually work, one

---

118 https://codeclub.org/en/ Accessed 30/01/22

119 Scratch https://scratch.mit.edu/about Accessed 30/01/22

little boy saying to me, "I'll remember these classes as long as I live".

Manchester tech companies also saw the need to influence 8 to 18-year-olds. Many contributed to community groups, including Girl Geeks, CoderDojo, Pi Club and HacJunior. These groups were mostly mixed girls and boys and adopted a workshop format developing practical skills and building confidence. As I had recently retired, I was keen to get involved as a mentor, refresh my programming skills and, alongside the children, learn new languages such as Python, Sonic Pi, Blender and physical computing with Raspberry Pi, Micro-Bit and the Arduino. There was a real sense of excitement about the Raspberry Pi, a computer the size of an iPhone, whose transparent casing enabled you to see the memory, processing unit and input/output connectors. No longer a 'black box', the computer was now accessible and much easier to understand.

The Girl Geeks group (mostly young women) was great fun. At one session we showed them how to write Scratch and a 15-year-old girl said, after successfully completing her program, "I never thought I could do this". She had her eureka moment and went away determined to learn more.

The HacJunior group occasionally ran all-girl sessions, lasting two whole days, where they worked in teams to solve problems set by local businesses. Each team had to understand the problem, design a solution, program it and then demonstrate the outcome. Typically, they were ten teams of five, aged 11 to 18 years old. Some parents seemed happier for their daughters to attend an all-girls event, rather than the mixed group; they dropped them off, then attended the demonstration and prize-giving at the end. Parents of the under-13s usually stayed throughout. It was such a treat for me to be among so many talented girls from across the region. Having spent most of my working life in a predominantly male environment, I found it refreshing and exciting.

I recall talking to one team of 16 to 17-year-olds and asking if they intended to apply for computer science at university. They all said, "no" – two had applied to do medicine, one biochemistry and one mathematics, all STEM subjects but not computing! This reflected the increasing trend of female participation in medicine and other science subjects, while their uptake of computer science was in decline.

Teachers, especially, lagged behind in their knowledge and experience of technology. Very few had experience of programming or computers of any kind, relying on a few self-taught enthusiasts. An initiative in 2010 sought to educate and change attitudes among teachers. Computing at Schools[120] mission was to educate and equip schoolteachers so that they could deliver computing across the curriculum.

In 2013, the UK government introduced a National Curriculum for Computing[121] for 5- to 16-year-olds; teaching how digital systems work and how to put this knowledge to use through programming. I was excited by their goal that students should be 'able to use, express themselves and develop their ideas through information and communication technology'.

Today, girls have as much exposure to computing as boys and as much opportunity to be active participants in the digital world.

BECOMING A WOMAN IN TECH

Would a woman in tech do anything different from a man in tech? A woman could do all the things a man could do but the key point is about the balance of power between male and female perspectives. It's about including a diversity of views in the purpose of new technologies, their design and how and why data is collected and analysed. The imbalance in perspectives

---

[120] https://www.computingatschool.org.uk/about# Accessed 30/02/22

[121] https://www.gov.uk/government/publications/national-curriculum-in-england-computing-programmes-of-study Accessed 30/01/22

leads to tech products more suited to male characteristics than female, for example see [18] [55] [17].

We need women to contribute to technology innovation by bringing a broader skillset and new perspective to human interaction with computers and to address the needs of wider society by shedding light on the bias inherent in Artificial Intelligence, historic data and algorithms.

We need more tech women to work their way up the career ladder so they can influence the rationale behind new technologies and be involved in design decisions. Stop the overarching design-by-men-for-men deep-rooted in the industry and shift the balance to design by men and women for the wider good of society and all our futures.

Is it any easier for women now? The #MeToo movement has made employers and individuals more aware of the harm that sexism can do both physically and mentally and punitive action taken within business and the courts should help women stand their ground. This together with changing attitudes of traditional male and female roles in society[122] should ensure greater recognition of a woman's equal technical and leadership capabilities.

Groups dedicated to encouraging participation now give women and girls a path through. For example, @CodeFirstGirls[123] partner with business 'to help more women gain the skills, confidence and tools they need to kick-start, revamp, or reignite their career in tech'. @GirlsWhoCode[124] is 'working to close the gender gap in technology by teaching girls computer science, bravery, and sisterhood.'

---

[122] British Social Attitudes Survey 2018:Gender https://www.bsa.natcen.ac.uk/media/39248/bsa35_gender.pdf Accessed 30/01/22

[123] https://codefirstgirls.org.uk/about-us/ Accessed 30/01/22

[124] https://girlswhocode.com Accessed 30/01/22

After years of frustration with seeing little change for Women in Tech, Gillian Arnold and colleagues produced an excellent book [67] providing practical guidance to employers and digital leaders on how to tackle the gender imbalance. There really is no excuse.

Women in Tech helps raise the profile of the many inspirational women in tech today[125]. Here are three of them together with their advice for girls and young women today:

"Recognize and embrace your uniqueness…being a black woman, being a woman in general, on a team of all men, means that you are going to have a unique voice. It's important to embrace that." Erin Teague, Director of Product Management at YouTube[126].

"Always be curious, always learn, don't worry about not getting it right first time, build your network, reach out to more senior women, and find something you enjoy"[127] Sarah Greasley, Chief Technology Officer at Direct Line Group.

"I started with a placement in the IT department and now manage a large Tech team of developers building applications for the media industry and big movie studios." Katie Nykanen, Chief Technology Officer at Adstream.

Katie has no doubts "Technology is the future….. why would you want to be anywhere else….???"[128]

---

[125] https://www.womenintech.co.uk Accessed 30/01/22

[126] https://computerhistory.org/profile/erin-teague/ Accessed 30/01/22

[127] https://www.womenintech.co.uk/direct-line-group-sarah-greasley-chief-technology-officer Accessed 30/01/22

[128] https://www.womenintech.co.uk/adstream-katie-nykanen-cto Accessed 30/01/22

Finally

When I first started this memoir, I thought I would focus on how computers have changed during my lifetime, discussing what they were like in the 1970s, 1980s etc each decade for the past fifty years. I wanted to show the ever-accelerating rate of change and at the same time show that many of the underlying concepts remain the same. It was my intention to educate the lay person - those with little computing knowledge - about how computers work and how software is designed and written.

My life's passion is Human Computer Interaction and how we can design systems that take the human into account at every stage in the software development process.

I tried to show what it was like working with computers and real-life problems and how the advent of new technologies brought and continues to bring new opportunities. Exploring the possible through interaction with people and through academic research has been my privilege.

I have focussed on my own experience with computers and as such do not pretend that this is a history of computing. There are others whose professional lives are dedicated to this complex and wide-ranging subject, Martin Campbell-Kelly for example [4].

I positioned each chapter in the socio-economic context of the time to show the everchanging landscape that is the backdrop to new technology. At the beginning of my story big computer companies were in their infancy and the balance of power between large corporations, governments and citizens was biased towards governments. The terror attack of 9/11 brought massive technological change, the digital infrastructure of the cloud brought access to memory and processing power into our personal computers, laptops and smart phones and gave businesses potentially unlimited access to computing resources. Companies who collect vast swathes of data via the internet now know more than governments about their own citizens.

Tim Berners-Lee gave us the web and free access to communicate with the world. Initially it felt like the Wild West, a parallel world without governance. In many ways it doesn't feel that much different now; we all have to be on our guard. Berners-Lee's vision that the internet be owned by everyone is being challenged but he and the World Wide Web Foundation continue to fight to establish open access to the web as a basic human right and as a public good. The advent of social media has added to the imbalance of power and control in favour of the big five corporations - Google, Apple, Microsoft, Amazon and Facebook – in the west. This shift in the balance of power has significantly changed the computing landscape and there is now an overriding need for ordinary people to take control.

I did start the memoir with a view to discussing the interaction between people and computers and how experiments conducted as part of my research career link to developments today. For example, in early work we called on behavioural sciences to inform the design of user interfaces and adapt them to the way individuals think (cognitive style). We measured user performance through monitoring every keystroke - our experiments were carried out in a laboratory without connection to the internet. Today individual preferences are gleaned constantly from data gathered online and keystroke monitoring is widespread, for example to measure the performance of call centre staff or the level of activity of those working-from-home.

Our work on privacy and security is as relevant today as it was then with increasing need for individuals and organisations to protect themselves online no longer just from individual hackers but from seriously well organised cyber criminals.

I have found it surprising, given my own experiences of virtual worlds and research into collaborative working, that more use hasn't been made of these technologies to create enriched meeting places for geographically dispersed teams. Metaverses are now emerging, that is, immersive, video-game-like virtual reality environments that we will no doubt come to inhabit as part of our everyday lives.

I didn't expect to write so much about women in computing. I'd always thought I just needed to be the best I could, an expert in my subject, and I would progress through my career. I was never naive enough to believe we lived in a fair meritocracy and knew I had to be political and strategic about the choices I made.

I totally underestimated the impact that being a woman would have. Once I started reflecting, I realised just how much prejudice existed and how accepting I had been of the status quo. I took for granted my right to be exceptional in my success when in fact what I achieved should be the norm. Women shouldn't have to strive harder than men.

I now realise how much my progression depended on support from the state and local government. As a child my mother received a widow's allowance to help support her four children after my father's death. At age eleven I attended a state-sponsored grammar school where I was introduced to my first computer. At age eighteen I was able to go to university despite our family having no money - at the time only 7% of the population went to university and the government sought to increase access to all by not charging fees. If we had had to pay fees then I'm sure I wouldn't have been able to go. In addition, the local authority gave me a means-tested living allowance to pay for books and accommodation. At twenty-one I won a scholarship from the state sponsored Science Research Council to study for a postgraduate degree at St. Andrews. As a working class girl, would I have made so much progress without the support of the state?

I didn't expect to write so much about my personal life. I've always been a private person keeping my feelings to myself and as a woman in a man's world have learnt that it's usually best not to share too much of yourself. Rather stick to work-related conversations.

Through writing about my personal life, I realise that this is really a love story. I met Patrick when I was eighteen and not a day has passed when I wasn't excited to see him. This isn't Patrick's memoir, he is a very different person to me - independent, free-thinking, artistic - and has his own story to tell.

Everyone has a story to tell, mine is of a life empowered by working with computers. Computers that have enhanced people's lives, made a difference to the effectiveness of organisations however small and most fun of all writing software to make something out of nothing. As well as technical skills in computer programming and design, I have had to be creative in bringing forward new ideas, develop problem solving and analytical skills, while at the same time think about the ethics of my actions/decisions. Bringing together an understanding of people with technical know-how has been immensely rewarding.

All our futures will be influenced by technology, technology designed by humans - hopefully all kinds of humans not just men. Life as a woman in tech may still be a challenge but the more of us there are the more enlightened our world will be. Technology changes constantly but fundamentally humans don't change that much and no matter what your interest: medical, financial, pharmaceutical, astronomy, forestry, weather or the earth's ecosystem, there will always be opportunities and challenges that tech can help you solve.

'What makes a life? More than what we say; more even than what we do. A life is also what we love and what we believe in .'
Edward Snowden [68]

Works Cited

1. S. McKay, The Secret Life of Bletchley Park: The WW11 Codebreaking Centre and the Men and Women Who Worked There, Autum Press, 2011.

2. R. Anderson, "historyandpolicy," 08 February 2016. [Online]. Available: http://www.historyandpolicy.org/policy-papers/papers/university-fees-in-historical-perspective. [Accessed 3 October 2019].

3. P. J. Denning, "Virtual Memory," Computing Surveys, vol. 2, no. 3, pp. 154-189, 1970.

4. M. Campbell-Kelly, W. Asprey, N. Ensmenger and J. Yost, Computer: A History of the Information Machine, Boulder, Colorado: Westview, 2014.

5. M. H. MacDougall, "Computer System Simulation: An Introduction," Computing Surveys, vol. 2, no. 3, pp. 191-209, 1970.

6. D. W. Simborg, L. K. Macdonald, J. S. Liebman and P. Musco, "Ward information-management system - An evaluation," Computers and Biomedical Research, vol. 5, no. 5, pp. 484-497, 1972.

7. J. Martin, Programming Real-time Computer Systems, Englewood Cliffs, NJ: Prentice-Hall, 1965.

8. J. Abbate, Recoding Gender: Women's Changing Participation in Computing, Cambridge, Massachusetts: MIT Press, 2012.

9. S. Shirley, Let IT Go, Luton: Andrews UK Limited, 2013.

10. E. Edmonds, "Adaptive Man-Computer Interfaces," in Computing Skills and the User Interface, London, Academic Press, 1981.

11. H. Witkin and D. Goodenough, Cognitive Styles: Essence and Origins, New York: International University Press, 1981.

12. H. Witkin, P. Oltman, E. Raskin and S. Karp, A manual for the Group Embedded Figures Test, Menlo Park, California: Mind Garden Inc, 1971.

13. M. Hicks, Programmed Inequality: How Britain discarded women technologists and lost its edge in computing, MIT Press, 2018.

14. S. Schuman, The IAF Handbook of Group Facilitation, San Francisco: Jossey-Bass, 2005.

15. T. Berners-Lee and M. Fischetti, Weaving The Web: The Past, Present and Future of the World Wide Web by its Inventor, London: Orion Business, 1999.

16. M. Budig, "The Fatherhood Bonus and the Motherhood Penalty," Third Way, 2014. [Online]. Available: http://content.thirdway.org/publications/853/NEXT_-_Fatherhood_Motherhood.pdf. [Accessed June 2020].

17. A. Adam, Artificial Knowing, London: Routledge, 1998.

18. C. C. Perez, Invisible Women : Exposing Data Bias in a World Designed for Men, London: Chatto & Windus, 2019.

19. L. Macaulay, Human Computer Interaction for Software Designers, International Thomson Computer Press, 1995, pp. 1-222.

20. G. O'Hare, P. Dongha, L. Macaulay and S. Viller, "Agency within CSCW: Towards the development of active co-operative working environments," in CSCW and Artificial Intelligence, Springer-Verlag, CSCW Series, 1995, pp. 65-95.

21. L. Macaulay, G. O'Hare, S. Viller and P. Dongha, "Cooperative Requirements Capture: Prototype Evaluation," in Computer Support for Co-operatiive Work, John Wiley & Sons, 1994, pp. 169-195.

22. L. Macaulay, "Requirements as a Co-operative Activity," in First IEEE Conference on Requirements Engineering, RE 93, San Diego, California, 1993.

23. M. Pohl, "The Internet - a 'feminine' technology?," in Women in Computing, Exeter, Intellect Books, 1997.

24. T. Berners-Lee, Weaving the Web, London: Orion Business, 1999.

25. L. Macaulay, "The role of the facilitator in distributed teamwork (with specific reference to Requirements Engineering teams)," Doctoral thesis, University of Manchester, 1997.

26. L. Macaulay, Requirements Engineering, Springer-Verlag London Limited, 1996.

27. L. Macaulay, "Requirements for Requirements Engineering Techniques," in IEEE International Conference on Requirements Engineering, Colorado Springs, 1996.

28. L. Macaulay and S. S. Salim, "Groupware: What you see is what you need?," in 7th International Conference on Human Computer Interaction, San Francisco, USA, 1997.

29. K. Hawton, L. Harriss, S. Simkin, E. Jusczak, L. Appleby, R. McDonnell, T. Amos, K. Kiernan and H. Parrott, "Effect of death of Diana, Princess of Wales, on suicide and deliberate self-harm," British Journal of Psychiatry, vol. Nov, no. 177, pp. 463-466, 2000.

30. L. Howe-Walsh and S. Turnbull, "Barriers to women leaders in academia: tales from science and technology," Journal of Studies in Higher Education, no. June, pp. 415-428, 2014.

31. G. Santos and S. Phu, "Gender and Academic Rank in the UK," Sustainability, vol. 11, no. 3171, pp. 1-46, June 2019.

32. P. Layzell and L. Macaulay, "An Investigation into Software Maintenance - Perception and Practices," Journal of Software Maintenance: research and practice, vol. 6, no. 3, pp. 105-120, 1994/5.

33. P. Brereton, D. Budgen, K. Bennett, M. Munro, P. Layzell, L. G. D. Macaulay and C. Stannet, "The Future of Software," Communications of the ACM, vol. 42, no. 12, pp. 78-84, 1 December 1999.

34. P. Brereton, S. Lees, M. Gumbley, C. Boldeyreff, S. Drummond, P. Layzell, L. Macaulay and R. Young, "Distributed Group

Working in Software Engineering Education," Information and Software Technology, vol. 40, no. 4, pp. 221-227, 5 July 1998.

35. L. Macaulay, K. Keeling, P. McGoldrick, G. Dafoulas, M. Kalaitzakis and D. Keeling, "Co-evolving E-tail and Online Communities: Empirically Based Conceptual Framework," International Journal of e-Commerce, vol. 11, no. 4, pp. 53-77, 2007.

36. B. Castle, Fighting All The Way, London: Macmillan, 1993.

37. E. Pankhurst, Suffragette: The Autobiography of Emmeline Pankhurst, kindle reproduction: Hearst's International Library Co., 1914.

38. J. Abbate, Recoding Gender: Women's Changing Participation in Computing, Cambridge, Massachusetts: The MIT Press, 2012.

39. R. Jungk and N. Mullert, Future Workshops: How to Create Desirable Futures, London: Institute for Social Inventions, 1987.

40. L. Macaulay, Requirements Engineering, London: Springer, 1996.

41. R. Adam, A Woman's Place 1910-1975, London: Persephone Books, 1975.

42. E. Healey, Wives of Fame: Mary Livingstone, Jenny Marx and Emma Darwin, Bloomsbury Reader.

43. K. Keeling, P. McGoldrick, S. Beatty and L. Macaulay, "Face Value? Customer views of appropriate formats of embodied conversational agents (ECAs) in online retailing," in

Proceedings of 37th Hawaii International Conference on Systems Sciences, 2004.

44. F. Nachira, A. Nicolai, P. Dini, M. Le Louarn and L. R. Leon, "European Commission Digital Business Ecosystems," Luxembourg: Office for Official Publications of the European Communities, 2007. [Online]. Available: http://www.digital-ecosystems.org/dbe-book-2007. [Accessed june 2020].

45. Y. Tan and L. Macaulay, "Adoption of ICT among small businesses: vision versus reality," International Journal of Electronic Commerce, vol. 5, no. 2, pp. 188-203, 2007.

46. L. Macaulay, K. Keeling, D. Keeling, C. Mitchell and Y. Tan, "Using Virtual World Technology to Deliver Educational Services," in Case Studies in Service Innovation, New York, Springer Science+Business, 2012, pp. 125-129.

47. A. Kanamgotov, L. Kosht and M. P. S. Conrad, "User-Avatar Association in Virtual Worlds," in IEEE International Conference on Cyberworlds, 2014.

48. J. Gillard and N. Okonjo-Iweala, Women and Leadership, Penguin Random House UK, 2020.

49. M. Obama, Becoming Michelle Obama, New York: Penguin Random House, 2018.

50. S. Sandberg, Lean In: Women, Work, and the Will to Lead, London: Penguin Random House, 2015.

51. S. Wachter-Boettcher, Technically Wrong: Sexist apps, biased algorithms and other threats of toxic tech, New York, London: W.W. Norton and Company, 2017.

52. H. Fry, Hello World: How to be Human in the Age of the Machine, London: Transworld Publishers, Penguin Random House UK, 2019.

53. M. Kearns and A. Roth, the ethical algorithm, New York: Oxford University Press, 2020.

54. C. O'Neil, Weapons of Math Destruction: How nig data increases inequality and threatens democracy, Penguin, 2017.

55. V. Eubanks, Automating Inequality: How hig-tech tools profile, police and punish the poor, New York: Picador, 2019.

56. C. McDonald, "Percentage of women in tech remains low at 16% with little growth in 10 years," 4 Dec 2019. [Online]. Available: https://www.computerweekly.com/news/252474971/Percentage-of-women-in-tech-remains-low-at-16-with-little-growth-in-10-years. [Accessed 1 Dec 2020].

57. S. K. White, "Women in tech statistics: The hard truths of an uphill battle," 23 Jan 2020. [Online]. Available: https://www.cio.com/article/3516012/women-in-tech-statistics-the-hard-truths-of-an-uphill-battle.html. [Accessed 1 Dec 2020].

58. H. Devlin and A. Hern, "Why are there so few women in tech? The truth behind the Google memo," 8 Aug 2017. [Online]. Available:

https://www.theguardian.com/lifeandstyle/2017/aug/08/why-are-there-so-few-women-in-tech-the-truth-behind-the-google-memo. [Accessed 1 Dec 2020].

59. F. Richter, "GAFAM: Women still underrepresented in tech," 19 Feb 2020. [Online]. Available: https://www.statista.com/chart/4467/female-employees-at-tech-companies/. [Accessed 1 Dec 2020].

60. G. Rippon, Gendered Brain: the neuroscience that shatters the myth of the female brain, London: Bodley Head Ltd, 2019.

61. M. L. Shetterly, Hidden Figures, London: HarperCollins, 2016.

62. J. Margolis, Unlocking the Clubhouse: Women in Computing, MIT Press, 2003.

63. W. Wolfe-Herd, Make the First Move: Take Charge of Your Work, Love and Life, Penguin Portfolio, 2019.

64. S. Fowler, Whistleblower: My unlikely journey to Silicon Valley and speaking out against injustice, Penguin Books, 2021.

65. A. Wiener, Uncanny Valley: A Memoir, Fourth Estate, 2020.

66. K. O'Hara and W. Hall, Four Internets: Data, Geopolitics, and the Governance of Cyberspace, Oxford University Press, 2021.

67. G. Arnold, H. Dee, C. Herman, A. Palmer and S. Shah, Women in Tech: A practical guide to increasing gender diversity and inclusion, London: BCS, The Chartered Institute for IT, 2021.

68. E. Snowden, Permanent Record, London: Pan Books, 2020.

Appendix

Note on the Title

'Hello Computer' is one of the great moments from the 1986 science fiction film

Star Trek IV: The Voyage Home

Scotty travels back in time from 2286 to 1986 and assumes he can speak to the computer, an Apple Mac Plus, 'Hello Computer' he says repeatedly until he realises he has to use the keyboard and remarks 'a keyboard, how quaint' https://www.youtube.com/watch?v=QpWhugUmV5U

Example of a Fortran IV program

The Fortran IV program below calculates the area of a triangle using Heron's formula (Named after Hero of Alexandria - the formula is used when the length of the three sides of the triangle are known but not the height)

For a triangle with sides of length a, b and c

First calculate 's' (where s is half the triangles perimeter) s = (a+b+c)/2

Then calculate the Area A = Square Root (s(s-a)(s-b)(s-c))

The program below reads in values for a, b and c calculates the Area and prints/writes it out

It continues in a loop reading new values for a, b and c, and printing/writing the Area until the values input for a, b and c are all given as zero – then the program stops.

If any of the values of a or b or c are zero then it prints/writes 'input error' – then the program stops.

Example taken from Wikibooks (open books for an open world) https://en.wikibooks.org/wiki/Fortran/Fortran_examples#Simple_Fortran_IV_program

Multiple data card input

This program has two input checks: one for a blank card to indicate end-of-data, and the other for a zero value within the input data. Either condition causes a message to be printed.

```
C AREA OF A TRIANGLE - HERON'S FORMULA
C INPUT - CARD READER UNIT 5, INTEGER INPUT, ONE BLANK CARD FOR END-OF-DATA
C OUTPUT - LINE PRINTER UNIT 6, REAL OUTPUT
C INPUT ERROR DISPAY ERROR MESSAGE ON OUTPUT
  501 FORMAT(3I5)
  601 FORMAT(4H A= ,I5,5H  B= ,I5,5H  C= ,I5,8H  AREA= ,F10.2,
     $13H SQUARE UNITS)
  602 FORMAT(10HNORMAL END)
  603 FORMAT(23HINPUT ERROR, ZERO VALUE)
      INTEGER A,B,C
   10 READ(5,501) A,B,C
      IF(A.EQ.0 .AND. B.EQ.0 .AND. C.EQ.0) GO TO 50
      IF(A.EQ.0 .OR.  B.EQ.0 .OR.  C.EQ.0) GO TO 90
      S = (A + B + C) / 2.0
      AREA = SQRT( S * (S - A) * (S - B) * (S - C) )
      WRITE(6,601) A,B,C,AREA
      GO TO 10
   50 WRITE(6,602)
      STOP
   90 WRITE(6,603)
      STOP
      END
```

Acknowledgements

I have enjoyed writing this book but couldn't have done it without the support and encouragement of a whole bunch of people. I particularly want to acknowledge family members who have commented on early drafts and who put me right on a few facts: Patrick, Sheila, Theresa, Christine, Zach, Joan and David.

Jeanette Chalmers got me started on the memoir and encouraged me to join the Manchester Women Writers group who generously commented week by week as my writing developed 'Keep going Linda, just keep writing!' they would say - spurring me on to translate my passion into words. My thanks to all but especially Susan, Karen, Helen, Margaret, Carole, Katie, Anne, Colette, Mimmi, Jan, Ruth and Linda K.

Thank you to those brave people who reviewed drafts of the whole book giving invaluable feedback Yin Leng Tan, Ann Gledson, George Dafoulas, Aida Azadegan, Mauricette Scheurer, Sarah Hinchliffe and Vicky Buck who commented 'You have all the right words Linda, but in the wrong order'. I am eternally grateful.

My writing coach, Judi Goodwin who through our monthly sessions inspired me to get to the heart of the matter 'What do you really want to say?' - coached me in the art of writing and cajoled me into expressing emotions not just facts.

I acknowledge the many inspirational women and men whose books are cited throughout - their memoirs, investigations, revelations and technical excellence have given me courage.

Finally, not to forget Adam Allsuch Boardman whose illustrations have kept me entertained.

Thank you all.

Linda